THE
PITCHING
CLINIC

THE PITCHING CLINIC

John Stewart

Illustrations by George Henry

BURFORD BOOKS

Printed in Canada

10 9 8 7 6 5 4 3 2 1

Library of Congress Cataloging-in-Publication Data
Stewart, John, 1964–
    The pitching clinic / John Stewart.
        p.   cm.
    Includes index.
    ISBN 1-58080-098-X (pb)
    1. Pitching (Baseball).   I. Title.
GV871.S69   2002
796.357'22—dc21   2001008680

CONTENTS

INTRODUCTION

Whether you are the occasional baseball fan or a major-league manager, there is one thing that you can certainly agree on: Pitching is the single most important part of baseball. A team cannot win consistently without good pitching. All coaches will tell you they never have enough pitching and are always looking for more.

Pitching, although complicated, can be taught. There are some basic mechanics that must be mastered, but any players who have some arm strength and a willingness to listen can become good pitchers. The following pages will explain in detail the do's and don'ts of pitching through pictures and diagrams. After you understand the basics, it is very important to practice the mechanics and master as many as possible. You don't need to master all the mechanics to be a successful pitcher, but the more you can master, the better you will be.

I will bring this point up more than once in this book, but I cannot express strongly enough the importance of throwing the fastball. Seventy percent of balls thrown by a pitcher should be fastballs. The young pitcher—age 13 and under—should throw nothing but fastballs. Off-speed pitches are very straining on the arm; young pitchers have a very high probability of arm injury if they attempt off-speed pitches.

One other note: The information discussed in the following pages will be best utilized by the reader with some basic knowledge of pitching. My previous book, *The Baseball Clinic,* discusses the fundamentals of pitching from a beginner's perspective. Although *The Pitching Clinic* recaps basic techniques, the purpose of this book is to advance the reader beyond these fundamentals. The reader who has not read *The Baseball Clinic* will find it worthwhile to review that book before moving on to *The Pitching Clinic.*

Let's get started. And the best way to start is at the beginning.

1

Basic
Technique

Fastball Grip

The grip on the fastball controls the action of the pitch. Based on the grip, a pitcher can make the ball run, sink, run and sink, cut, or stay straight. For the young pitcher new to the pitching mound, I strongly recommend finding one grip that is effective and staying with it to develop a consistent strike pitch. As the pitcher develops his ability to throw consistent strikes, he can experiment with other grips.

BASIC GRIPS

- **With the seams** (see Figure 1): This grip is executed by putting the index and middle fingers along the seams at the point on the ball where the seams are closest together. Look at a baseball: The writing is between the seams that are needed to properly throw this pitch. This grip will give the ball a running action, which means that instead of traveling in a straight line to the plate, it will have a tendency to move into a right-handed hitter or away from a left-hander if thrown by a right-handed pitcher. For the left-handed pitcher, the ball will move away from a right-handed hitter and into a left-hander. Usually this pitch will not change plane. Keeping the fingers close together (rather than spread apart) will produce more action. If

Figure 1. With-the-seams grip

this pitch is thrown low in the strike zone, it will have a tendency to sink. It is quite possible to make this pitch run and sink if a pitcher has proper mechanics and a strong arm (see Figures 2 and 3).

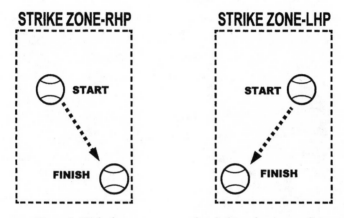

Figure 2. With-the-seams run and sink (view from mound)

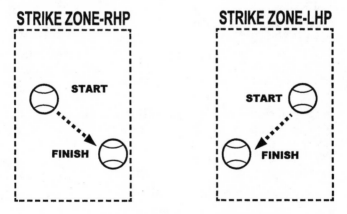

Figure 3. Two-seam run (view from mound)

- **Across the seams** (see Figure 4): This grip is executed by putting the index and middle fingers over the seams instead of parallel to the seams. In this grip, the seams can be held on any section as long as the fingertips are on a seam and the fingers are across a set of seams. The most important point of the grip—also referred to as the four-seam fastball—is the fingertips touching a seam. This pitch usually will be fairly straight in action. It is used when a pitcher is trying to throw the ball to a specific point in the strike zone and does not want the ball to have any additional unexpected movement in flight. This grip is also recommended to all position players throwing across the infield or in from the outfield, because its movement is very limited. If a pitcher throws at a high velocity, the ball will seem to explode at the plate—it appears to pick up speed as it approaches the plate. There is a chance the pitch may have some running action, but this should be limited (see Figure 5). Just as in the with-the-seams grip, keep the fingers close together and try to keep the ball on the fingertips (see Figure 6).

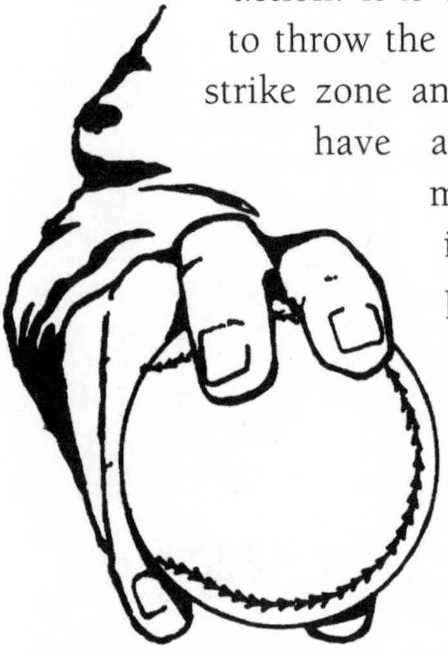

Figure 4.
Across-the-seams grip

A young pitcher with small hands will struggle gripping the ball on his fingertips. Do not force the fingertip grip; just be sure the ball is held with the correct seams.

4

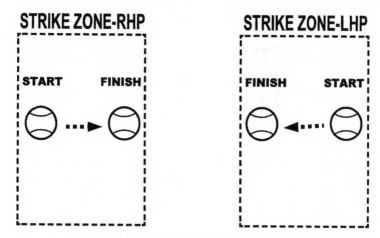

Figure 5. Four-seam action (view from mound)

The young pitcher may have to grip the ball with three fingers because his hands are too small. Both grips can be performed with three fingers. Be sure to encourage the two-finger grip as soon as physically possible, however, because the third finger will reduce velocity.

When first attempting these grips, the most important consideration is comfort. Have the pitcher try both grips and decide which is easier to control, and which is more natural to the hand. Do not vary grips when first attempting them. Give the pitcher enough opportunity to decide which grip feels better before alternating grips.

Figure 6. Fingers too close together

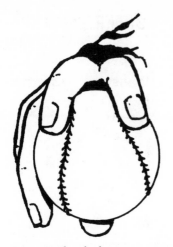

Figure 7. Thumb placement directly between fingers

In all grips, the thumb should be directly under the ball between the index and middle fingers. The thumb should not be on the side of the ball or bent at the knuckle (see Figure 7).

Choice of grip has little effect on velocity. If there is any advantage to speed, the four-seam fastball gives the appearance of being faster. Keep in mind that movement is much more effective in getting hitters out than speed. Movement and control are a pitcher's main goals. Learning how to throw strikes to all sections of the strike zone is much more important than velocity.

Here are some important points to watch for when properly throwing a fastball:

• **Staying behind the ball:** Be sure the pitcher keeps his hand and fingers behind the ball at release. Often a young pitcher will let his hands turn onto the side of the ball at release. This will cause the ball to come out of his hand spinning side-to-side instead of end-over-end (see Figure 8).

• **Full extension:** Make sure the pitcher releases the ball with his arm fully extended to the plate. Often the pitcher will let the ball go before full extension, resulting in a loss of velocity because the ball is traveling farther (see Figure 9).

- **Maximum arm speed:** Many a pitcher will slow his arm down to throw strikes. This seems to make sense, but in reality the problem throwing strikes comes earlier in the motion. Encourage the pitcher to use maximum arm speed and correct other problems separately.

Figure 8. Stay behind the ball

- **Cutting the ball off:** This problem occurs when a pitcher stops his arm action after the release. Often this is done to see where the ball is going or to field his position. A pitcher should naturally let his arm slow down—but not stop it quickly for any reason. Such cutting off can lead to a serious arm injury. Some pitchers try to watch the pitch from release to the catcher's mitt; this will also cause a pitcher to cut his throw off. If the ball is thrown properly, the

Figure 9. Full arm extension

pitcher will lose sight of it for a split second. Be sure to reach as far as possible at release.

It is important for the young pitcher to learn to throw strikes. Giving the ball velocity and life are of little importance if he does not throw strikes. Encourage him to aim at the middle of the strike zone and become accurate with his throw, rather than moving the target all around the strike zone and using many grips.

The windup and delivery are the actions a pitcher takes before he delivers the ball to the plate. There are many parts to a conventional delivery and windup, each of which has a specific purpose. Performing any of these elements incorrectly will cause some sort of problem with either control or velocity. I will now break down the whole process, from the pitcher walking onto the mound through the release. Keep in mind that all parts of this process play a role in a successfully pitched ball. I will also tell you what happens if a move is done incorrectly; this should help pinpoint the pitcher's most likely error, based on the result of the pitch.

Address

The *address* is the process of the pitcher standing on the mound looking in at the catcher to find the target to which he will be throwing. At the advanced level, the pitcher may also receive signals from the catcher telling him what pitch to throw and what spot to hit (see Figure 10).

The pitcher should start the address by standing with both feet together on the rubber facing the catcher. He should not have his feet more than 4 or 5 inches apart. If his feet are too separated, he runs the risk of losing his balance

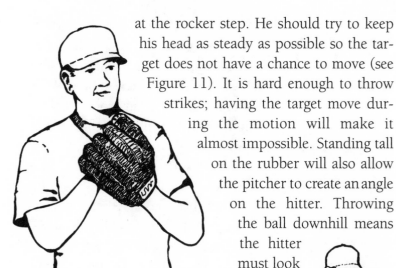

at the rocker step. He should try to keep his head as steady as possible so the target does not have a chance to move (see Figure 11). It is hard enough to throw strikes; having the target move during the motion will make it almost impossible. Standing tall on the rubber will also allow the pitcher to create an angle on the hitter. Throwing the ball downhill means the hitter must look up for the ball, so there is a better

Figure 10. The address

chance that the ball will miss the best part of the bat during the swing.

Foot positioning is also very important. The middle of the rubber (see Figure 12) is the best place to start for the young pitcher. It allows him to start in the middle of the strike zone and gives a larger margin of error on both sides of the plate. As the pitcher advances in his career, moving to the throwing-hand side of the rubber will help him create an angle to the hitter. This offers him a slight advantage when throwing off-speed pitches or when throwing inside to a hitter (see Figures 13–14).

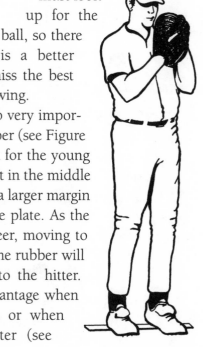

Figure 11. Stand tall

9

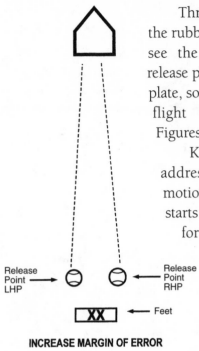

Release
Point
LHP

Release
Point
RHP

Feet

INCREASE MARGIN OF ERROR

Figure 12. Increase margin of error

Throwing from the wrong side of the rubber gives the hitter a chance to see the ball better: The pitcher's release point is from the middle of the plate, so the hitter can spot the ball in flight with minimal effort (see Figures 15–16).

Keep in mind that in the address position, the pitching motion has started. After a pitcher starts to deliver the ball, it is illegal for him to stop his motion.

Much confusion will result if the catcher and pitcher are not on the same page. At this point, both should know exactly what pitch is coming and where in the strike zone the ball should go. Finally, the pitcher should be focused on the pitch to be delivered. If his mind is wandering, he will not have much success.

A pitcher in the address position is prepared to start the windup to the plate. The next move is the rocker or pivot step.

Rocker Step

The *rocker step* is designed to start the transfer of body weight from the tall address position to the balance point. It is done by stepping one foot back behind the rubber. If a right-handed pitcher is on the mound, he will step back

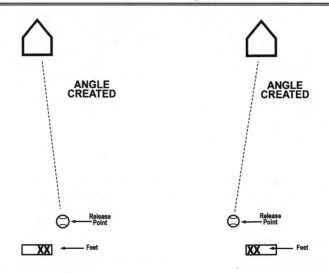

RIGHT-HANDED PITCHER

Figure 13. Right-handed pitcher rubber position

LEFT-HANDED PITCHER

Figure 14. Left-handed pitcher rubber position

WRONG SIDE—RHP

Figure 15. Incorrect starting point, right-handed pitcher

WRONG SIDE—LHP

Figure 16. Incorrect starting point, left-handed pitcher

with his left foot; a left-hander will step back with the right foot (see Figures 17–18). This only needs to be a small step—no more than 10 or 12 inches. Its purpose is to transfer the body weight from both feet to the back leg.

If the pitcher steps back too far, his head will move, changing the target. If the rocker step is too far to the left or right instead of straight back, he will allow his body to move toward first base (for the right-handed pitcher) or third base (for the left-hander). Either will again change the target area.

Figure 17. Correct rocker step, right-handed pitcher

Instead, keep the body and head still while transferring the weight back. At the same time, the hands should come together in the glove, grip the ball, and get the hands started into action. The hands can come together at the belt or chest—whichever is more comfortable. Both are optimum positions to get the hands prepared to start the throw. Occasionally a

Figure 18. Correct rocker step, left-handed pitcher

Figure 19. Hands over head in windup

pitcher may like to pick his hands up over his head. This is fine as long as his eyes are able to keep focused on the catcher's mitt (see Figure 19).

Next comes an intermediate step. The pitcher must turn his front foot—the one remaining on the rubber—into the area directly in front of the rubber. By rule, the foot needs to stay in contact with the rubber, but close to the rubber is allowed.

With all the pitcher's weight on his back leg, which is behind the rubber, turning the front foot should be easy. The right-handed pitcher's foot turn is in a clockwise direction; the left-hander's is counterclockwise. At the end of this action, the foot should be parallel to the rubber (see Figures 20–21). This move is referred to as the *pivot*.

The next move in the windup process is the leg kick.

Leg Kick

The *leg kick* is designed to let the pitcher get all his body weight onto his drive, or back, leg; this will help him gain velocity when throwing. If done correctly, the pitcher will be able to use the strength of his arm and most or all of his body weight in a thrust to the plate with maximum velocity. From the rocker step—all the pitcher's weight is on his back leg—he needs to throw that weight back onto his front foot, which is in front of and parallel to the rubber. When the back leg pushes the body weight forward, it allows the front foot to accept the weight. Now the back leg will be lifted up with the knee bent. The leg will kick up parallel to the rubber. The

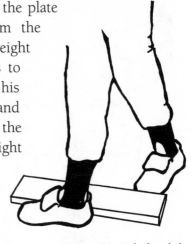

Figure 20. Right-handed pitcher pivot

right-handed pitcher will kick toward third base, the left-hander toward first (see Figures 22–23). The kick allows the pitcher to rotate his hips as well as form a balance point in preparation for the throw. At this point the hands should still be together with a proper grip on the ball.

The leg kick will vary in height depending on the pitcher. It is based on the arm action. For the pitcher who has a long arc, the leg kick should be higher, to allow enough time to complete the

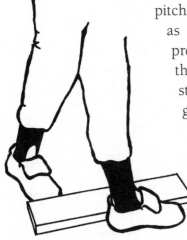

Figure 21. Left-handed pitcher pivot

arc. With a short quick arc, a lower leg kick will leave the body prepared when the arm is ready to throw. I will discuss proper arm action and landing later; for now, note that the throw needs to be made when the landing foot hits the ground. Thus, the arm action must be completed to the load point (see Figure 27) so that at landing, both arm and body are ready to throw. The only way any of this can happen is by using the leg kick to give both parts of the body time to get in position.

Figure 22. Leg kick-post, right-handed pitcher

The leg kick may be the easiest thing to fix or change in a pitcher's motion. It should be used as a timing mechanism for the entire windup and delivery. The main things to keep in mind are:

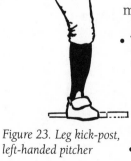

Figure 23. Leg kick-post, left-handed pitcher

- The length of the pitcher's arm action.
  - The length of the pitcher's arms.
    - The length of his stride.
    - The height at which he balances best.
- The height that is most comfortable.

A long-armed pitcher is more likely to have a long arm arc, and vice versa. A long-stride pitcher is less apt to need a high kick: His long stride will give his arm time. The most important part of the leg kick is gaining a balance point. Regardless of all the other factors involved, be sure the pitcher is able to find a solid balance point to work from.

The hands should not start to break until the leg is at the top of its kick. If the hands break too early, it will be very hard to get balanced. If they break too late, the body will complete the stride and landing before the arm is ready to throw.

Let me touch on the shoulder position during the leg kick. The pitcher should be attempting to get his shoulders level, with his front shoulder pointing directly at the catcher. If the shoulders are not level, it is hard to get a good view of the target. If the front shoulder is too high, the pitcher will struggle throwing downhill back to the strike zone. If it is too low, gaining leverage will be difficult. Level shoulders throughout the leg kick make it much easier to gain a solid balance point.

Now that we are at the top of the leg kick with a solid balance point and level shoulders, we should discuss the most important part of pitching.

Arm Action

Arm action is the single most determining factor in a pitcher's progress and success. Most pitching mechanics can be fixed with relative success. Most parts of the motion can be isolated and adjusted. The arm action is hard to revise, and if it is done wrong, it will cause many arm problems as well as command trouble.

Think of the arm as an engine. If the engine works incorrectly, it may run for a time, but it will malfunction before it normally should. Or it may show only occasional signs of problems, but will from time to time struggle and eventually quit. So it is with arm action. A pitcher can throw his whole career with improper arm action, but he has a chance to be a much better pitcher if he gets it right. He will also have less risk of injury.

Every person has his own individual arm action, but there are some points to remember to throw the ball with the maximum success and the least amount of arm exertion.

The arm action starts at the top of the leg kick. At the top of the kick, the hand and glove will separate; this is the beginning of the action. I will discuss only the throwing hand's action, not the glove hand's. When the hands break in the windup, the ball hand should come out of the glove and travel down below the waist, with the ball facing the ground and the back of the hand on top of the ball (see Figures 24–25). The arm should now develop a circle action, referred to as the *arc*. The distance that the arm and hand should travel below the waist is based on the length of the pitcher's arms and the specific pitcher throwing the ball. The only real requirement is that at some point, the ball gets slightly below the waist

Figure 24. Hand break, top of kick

(see Figure 25). From this point, the ball should move parallel to the ground and toward second base (see Figure 26). When the ball, hand, and arm have gotten to a point behind the body clear of the back leg, the arm should be lifted up over the head (see Figure 27). Be sure the back of the hand is between the head and the ball. The hand should always be between the pitcher's body and the ball. At no point in the arm action should the ball be clearly visible to the hitter; the hand should always interfere with the hitter's view of the ball.

The *load position* is reached when the arm, ball, and hand are all over the pitcher's head. At this point and this point

Figure 25. Hand traveling below waist

only the wrist should turn toward the plate, making the ball visible to the hitter, for it is time to propel the ball to the plate. Now the arm should head in the direction of the catcher's mitt. Be sure as the arm travels toward the plate that the elbow is even with or slightly above the throwing shoul-

Figure 26. Parallel to ground

der. The elbow should never drop below the throwing shoulder during the delivery. Now the arm should be picking up speed to get maximum velocity on the throw. If done correctly, the throwing hand is directly behind the ball (see Figure 28), still maintaining the desired grip. The pitcher should be looking directly at the target. If all these mechanics are executed correctly, the arm will have room to throw freely to the catcher's glove (see Figure 28).

Figure 27. Ball lifted over head to load point

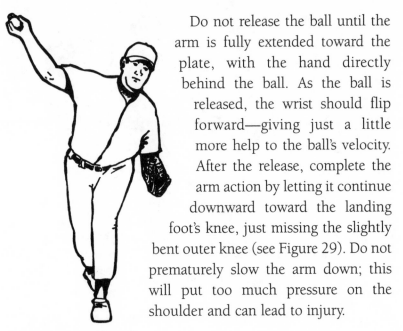

Do not release the ball until the arm is fully extended toward the plate, with the hand directly behind the ball. As the ball is released, the wrist should flip forward—giving just a little more help to the ball's velocity. After the release, complete the arm action by letting it continue downward toward the landing foot's knee, just missing the slightly bent outer knee (see Figure 29). Do not prematurely slow the arm down; this will put too much pressure on the shoulder and can lead to injury.

Figure 28. Head steady, arm has clear path

Figure 29. Ball released, arm finishing over knee

ARM-ACTION DO'S AND DON'TS

Do:

- Gain as much arm speed as possible.
- Keep the elbow even with or higher than the shoulder.
- Keep the back of the hand between the ball and the head.

- Be sure that the hand and ball break the plane of the waist in the arc.
- Let the arm develop a circle action behind the body.
- Release the ball at full extension.
- Get a wrist flip at release.
- Throw with the fingers in a proper grip behind the ball.

Don't:
- Turn the hand over too early in the arm action.
- Intentionally slow the arm after the release.
- Keep the throwing hand above the waist throughout the arm action.
- Let the throw occur without the hand and grip directly behind the ball.
- Throw with the elbow below the shoulder.

Most arm injuries occur because of improper arm positioning during the throwing process. The smoother the arm moves through the arm action, the less likely arm injuries become. Some arm problems are directly related to improper windup and delivery mechanics, but most are caused by improper arm action. It is much easier to correct the mechanics of the windup or delivery than it is the arm action. The solution is to teach proper arm action first and at a very young age to both pitchers and all position players. Nobody is above arm injuries.

Arm Angles

The arm action most often dictates what release point a pitcher will use. The *arm angle* is the point at which the ball is released toward the plate. The angles I will discuss almost all feature the elbow even with or above the shoulder. The exception is the submarine release point, which I will discuss only briefly. All of the following release points are acceptable, but the three-quarter to high three-quarter delivery is recommended, because it seems to put the least amount of strain on the arm and shoulder. The pitcher should choose a release point based on comfort and success.

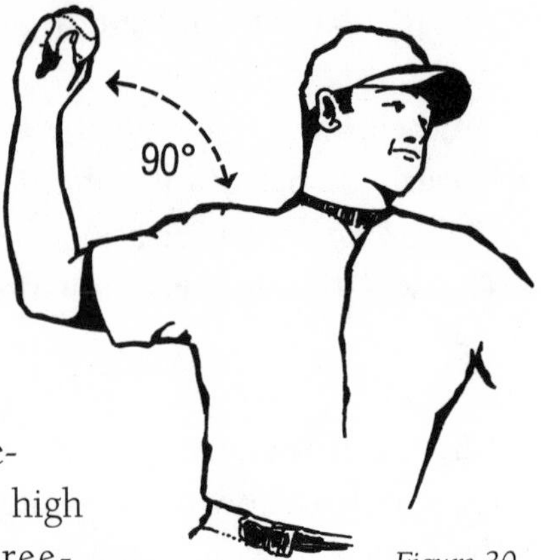

Figure 30. 90-degree angle

Figure 31. High three-quarter

• **Three-quarter:** The elbow is even with the shoulder and the hand is at a 90-degree angle from the shoulder, creating an L between the shoulder, elbow, and hand when heading for the plate (see Figure 30).

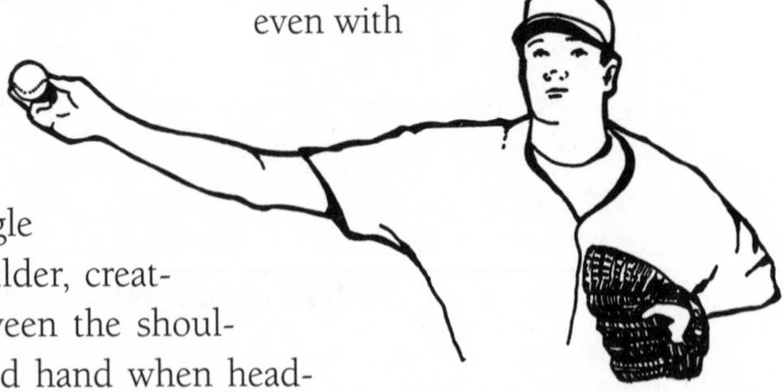

Figure 32. Low three-quarter

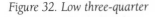

- **High three-quarter:** This angle is much like the three-quarter release, except the elbow is slightly higher, causing the hand to be just a few inches higher at release. This release is as common as the three-quarter (see Figure 31).

- **Low three-quarter:** This angle is also much like the three-quarter arm angle, except the elbow is slightly lower than the shoulder—but very close to even, as in the three-quarter delivery (see Figure 32).

Figure 33. Overhand

- **Overhand:** The elbow is much higher than the shoulder at release, and the hand is almost directly over the head when heading to the plate. Quite often, the pitcher will have to move his head to allow the arm to continue its action. A head tilt is easy to detect and a sure way to know that the pitcher is throwing overhand (see Figure 33).

Figure 34. Sidearm

- **Sidearm:** The pitcher extends his arm directly toward the corner base

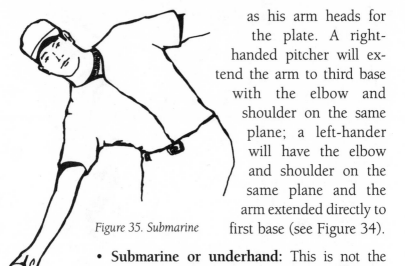

Figure 35. Submarine

as his arm heads for the plate. A right-handed pitcher will extend the arm to third base with the elbow and shoulder on the same plane; a left-hander will have the elbow and shoulder on the same plane and the arm extended directly to first base (see Figure 34).

• **Submarine or underhand:** This is not the same as an underhand softball throw. Here the pitcher never gets the elbow up to throw; instead, the arm extends toward the ground and develops a sweeping action with the hand coming back *up* to the catcher's mitt (a conventional throw is *down* to the mitt; see Figure 35).

The young pitcher should try to work on the three-quarter or high three-quarter release. It is fine for older pitchers to attempt other releases; still, they are more likely to cause arm problems. The young pitcher, with under-developed muscles, should try to stay away from the low three-quarter, sidearm, and submarine releases.

Balance Point

The *balance point* is the last part of the windup. It is one of the most important points, if not *the* most important, in the windup. Beyond the balance point, the remainder of the pitcher's action is called the delivery.

At the top of the leg kick, the arm is ready to break from the glove and prepare to throw the ball. If done correctly, the body weight of the pitcher is firmly placed on his back leg, which is parallel to the pitching rubber. At this balance point the pitcher should be at the highest point in his leg kick. He needs to feel all his body weight on his back leg. He should also feel as though he could stop the windup at this point and not fall off balance.

Figure 36. Correct post, weight back on inside back foot

At the top of the leg kick, the weight should be on the inner part of the back foot. If it is on any other part of the back foot, the pitcher will have a hard time driving to the plate (see Figures 36–37). Having the weight slightly forward of the rubber is acceptable, but if it is falling to first or third it needs to be corrected. At no time should the weight be falling to second base.

Figure 37. Incorrect post, weight on toe

The pitcher is at this point preparing to throw the ball and thrust his body toward the plate.

If the body is not perfectly balanced, it will be difficult to get the maximum push to the plate, and also to make an accurate throw to the catcher's mitt. On occasion this balance point is bypassed: With runners on base a pitcher may decide to slide step. I will discuss this later.

Before I continue, I need to stress the importance of direction. This is one of the most common problems in a pitcher's delivery, and it often goes undetected.

Direction is critical in throwing strikes.

Figure 38. Proper direction of stride foot

Figure 39. Too open

If the body does not move from the balance point toward the plate in a compact, quick action, many mechanical problems will occur. From the top of the leg kick, the foot should head directly toward the plate without any extra action. The foot should not stray from an imaginary route in the center of the plate. As the foot strides toward the plate, the arm should be nearing the release point (see Figures 38–40).

The Break

To this point we have talked about where the body should be in the windup. We have reached the top of the leg kick, and it is time to get the arm action started. At the top of the leg kick, the hands should separate. The throwing hand will take the ball out of the glove and start the arc. If the hands wait any longer, the arm might not get to the load point in time to throw; if the hand break has already happened,

Figure 40. Throwing across the body

the body will not get to the landing in time to throw the ball correctly (refer back to Figures 24–25).

At the break point, the front arm should extend toward the plate. This will serve as a point-of-sight reference, as well as helping keep the shoulders closed (see Figure 41). The glove will reach full

Figure 41. Extended front arm

extension toward the plate as the arm action nears the load position. This extension will help the pitcher keep his hips closed and coiled, giving him maximum use of his upper body.

I have discussed the entire windup, and have now incorporated the arm action and break. Let's return to the delivery.

Figure 42. Pulling front arm in

Stride Landing

The *stride* is the process of getting from the top of the leg kick and balance point to the ground prepared to throw. During the process of striding, the front arm, which is fully extended toward the plate, should now be pulled back into the hip (see Figure 42).

This will allow the body to rotate at the

Figure 43. Back leg finishing over landing leg

hips to clear an area out in front for the arm to throw toward the plate. The harder the front arm is able to pull back to the waist, the quicker the upper body will rotate. This helps the pitcher get more velocity from his upper body.

Here are some do's and don'ts of striding.

Do:

• Land on the balls of the feet.

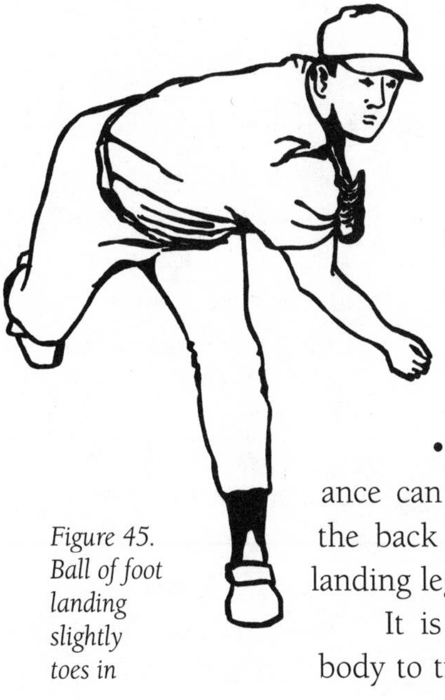

Figure 44. Flat-footed landing

Landing flat-footed is acceptable, but not recommended (see Figures 44–45).

Figure 45. Ball of foot landing slightly toes in

• Land so the front knee is slightly bent (see Figures 44–45).

• Land at a distance that balance can be regained quickly, and so the back leg can be thrown over the landing leg (see Figure 43).

It is important to try to get the body to travel in the same direction as the throw; otherwise all the work put into getting a balance point is wasted.

Don't:

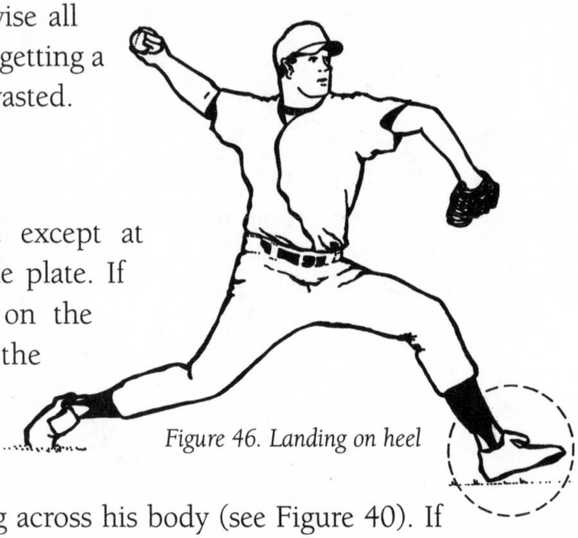

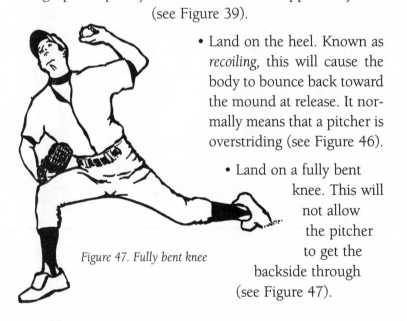

• Land anywhere except at the center of the plate. If the foot lands on the right side of the plate, a right-handed pitcher

Figure 46. Landing on heel

will be throwing across his body (see Figure 40). If it lands too far to the left, a right-handed pitcher is opening up too quickly and will not use his upper body well (see Figure 39).

• Land on the heel. Known as *recoiling,* this will cause the body to bounce back toward the mound at release. It normally means that a pitcher is overstriding (see Figure 46).

• Land on a fully bent knee. This will not allow the pitcher to get the backside through (see Figure 47).

Figure 47. Fully bent knee

• Land with-
out a break
in the front leg. The
pitcher will be too
upright with no flexibility (see
Figure 48).

*Figure 48. Too upright,
no break in knee*

The stride should transfer the body weight to the ground in one quick motion and add velocity on the throw. During the course of the stride, the weight that is left on the back leg should be pushed toward the plate, aiding in the stride. Push as hard as possible, using the leverage created from the back foot's placement against the rubber.

Here are some quick tips for detecting mistakes in the stride. If a pitcher understrides, he will throw low because his body is too upright. If he lands on his heel, his head will bounce and he will lose sight of the strike zone. If he lands on a knee that is too flexed, he will lose movement on his fastball as well as consistently throwing high, because he is throwing uphill.

When the landing foot hits the ground, it should land slightly closed (this is called the *toed-in position;* see Figure 45). This position helps the hips stay closed and allows the hips to explode toward the plate. It will also aid in gaining velocity. Although the foot lands toes in and on the ball, it will straighten to the plate as the hips rotate through the pitch.

Here is a more complete explanation of the "toed-in" or "slightly closed" foot position: The right-handed pitcher should land not pointed directly at the catcher's mitt or at the center of the plate; he should land pointed slightly at the right-handed batter's box (see Figure 45). The left-hander should have his toe pointed slightly at the left-handed batter's box. Landing with the foot pointed directly at the plate is not a problem—but the pitcher is not getting maximum use of his upper body. Do not land with the front foot pointed farther than the center of the plate. For instance, if the right-handed pitcher has his landing foot pointed at the left-handed batter's box, he will be opening up too early, causing a loss of velocity and control; vice versa for the left-hander. If either pitcher has his front foot too closed, he will throw across his body and will not be able to finish the release cleanly.

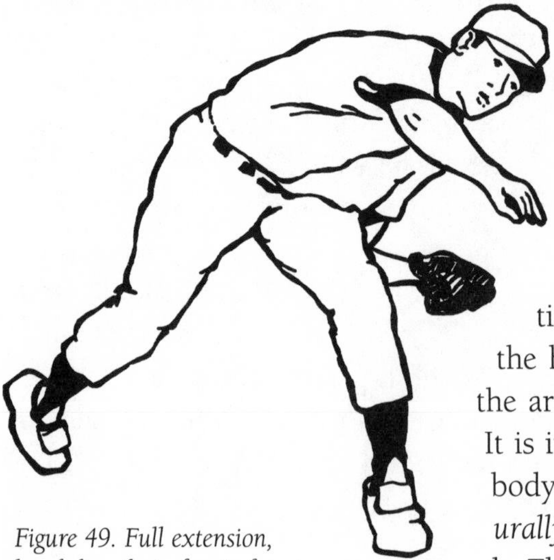

Figure 49. Full extension, hand directly in front of eyes

Release-Finish

The *finish* is the act of letting the ball out of the hand and slowing the arm without injury. It is important that the body slows down *naturally,* not prematurely. The back leg should

finish slightly in front of the landing foot. This
will ensure that the hips finish the pitch. The
pitcher should make
sure not to turn his
back after the throw,
in case the ball is hit
back up the middle.
If the ball is hit directly at him, he will need
to field it and make a
defensive play.

Figure 50.
Backside finish

If all parts of the windup
and delivery are done correctly or
even almost correctly, the finish will
happen naturally. Be sure to use a slight
wrist flip at the final release extension point. The
release should happen at full extension and no sooner. If it
comes early, the ball will have to travel farther, reducing
velocity and command. At full extension the pitcher releases the ball directly in front of his head—where his eyes have
never left the target (see Figure 49).

The finish should be completed without any extra
effort on the pitcher's part. If everything was done correctly,
he should be concerned only with the direction the ball is
hit (if it is hit). If he has to do anything to help the finish,
then his motion has a flaw.

2

Advanced
Pitches

Curveball

The curveball is much harder on a pitcher's arm than the fastball. It is not recommended for those age 14 and younger, who should learn to throw the fastball correctly and maybe experiment with the change-up, not the curveball.

The first thing to do in throwing the curveball is get a proper grip. The ball can be held in a number of different ways; the most important thing is comfort. I will discuss the two basic grips, but pitchers can experiment with small changes and variations to find what is most effective. Those presently gripping the fastball with the seams should hold the curveball the same way. Those who hold the fastball across the seams will need to make a slight change.

• **With-the-seams grip:** Hold the ball with the index and middle finger parallel to the seams; make sure the fingertips are touching the seams. Now move the middle finger ever so slightly, until it is just inside the seam. All parts of the middle finger should be on the inside edge of the seam. The finger should be in contact with the seam from approximately the middle knuckle all the way to the fingertip. This gives the middle finger added leverage on the ball, because it is in contact with the whole seam.

Now perform the pitching motion as usual. The only change in mechanics should be the grip. Some people think a curveball requires a change in arm action and release, but this is not true. Done correctly, it is basically the same as a fastball.

As the arm gets close to the release point, instead of keeping the hand behind the ball as with a fastball, the wrist should rotate from behind the ball in a top-to-bottom direction for both right- and left-handers (see Figure 51). This action will allow the fingers to come across the front of the ball and give the ball an *overspin*—spinning in a forward motion. (The fastball rotates end-over-end.) The fingers should not rotate side-to-side across the front of the ball (see Figure 52). If done correctly, the ball will rotate from the top down, giving it as much down rotation as possible.

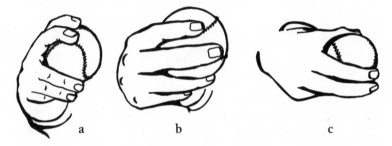

Figure 51. Proper wrist and finger action for curveball

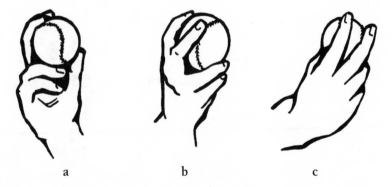

Figure 52. Incorrect side-to-side action for curveball

Figure 53. Hand on side of ball too early

The point at which the wrist should turn and the fingers rotate over the front of the ball is at full extension of the arm. The wrist should not rotate any earlier in the arm action (see Figure 53).

Another very important point to keep in mind is the finish. Just because the ball has left the hand does not mean the pitch is over. Keep moving the arm down through the front of the body. It should finish hard over the landing leg's knee and on the knee's outside (see Figure 54). A lazy or incomplete finish will not give the ball a tight hard break. The idea is not to make the ball spin and curve over a long distance, but rather to make it break at the latest point possible. This will disguise the pitch to the hitter.

The wrist should never bend during the arm action. It should stay stationary right up to the release. Then the wrist turn causes the fingers to rotate over the front of the ball. The ball should

Figure 54. Finish across front knee

come out of the hand between the thumb and the index finger (unlike the fastball, which rolls off the fingertips; see Figure 51c).

Keep in mind that the curveball needs to be thrown hard. Let the grip and the finger rotation take the speed off the ball. Trying to throw the curveball slower will allow the hitter to see the pitching arm slow down or make the ball curve over a long distance. Both will give the hitter a better chance. Try to throw the curveball directly at the catcher's mitt, and let it break away. Curveballs thrown to curve into the strike zone will not break sharply (see Figures 55–56). This is referred to as *hanging* or *casting the curveball*.

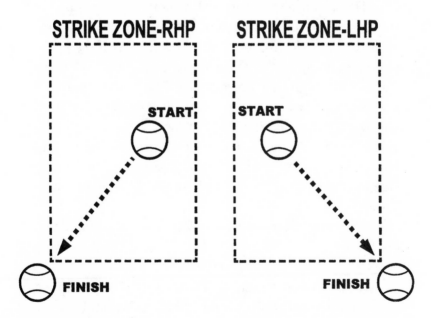

Figure 55. View from mound of curveball action, right-handed pitcher

Figure 56. View from mound of curveball action, left-handed pitcher

- **Across-the-seam grip:** Start by holding the ball across the seams like a fastball. Next, rotate the ball in the hand until the middle finger is tucked up against the seam. The seam should now be on the outside of the grip but in contact with the outside edge of the middle finger. This seam is used just as in the with-the-seams grip, for leverage.

The pitcher should try both of these grips and experiment with slight adjustments in them until he finds a comfortable and effective break. The later the break, the better. The ball needs to break only 6 inches to be a very effective pitch. If the curveball is thrown correctly, it should break across and down.

The action on the curveball is both a curve and sink action. The more end-over-end rotation a pitcher can provide, the more down action the ball will have. If the pitcher incorrectly spins the ball side-to-side, the ball will curve side-to-side, with little down action. The down action in a curveball is referred to as *depth* or *tilt.* The ideal curveball will break both side-to-side—by about 6 to 10 inches— and down 6 to 10 inches at the same time. This will be very hard for the hitter to hit or even make contact with. The side-to-side action is referred to as *sweep* or *cut,* and is much easier to hit.

The curveball is closely related to the slider and cutter.

Slider

All pitchers use basically the same grip on the slider. Looking at the ball, find the point where the seams form the letter U (see Figures 57–58). Hold the ball with the middle finger against the outside seam. For the right-handed pitcher, the middle finger should be against the right seam with the seam on the outside or right side of the finger (see Figures 57–58). The left-hander needs his middle finger against the left seam, again with the seam on the outside of the finger. This grip is identical to the across-the-seams curveball grip explained earlier.

Sometimes a pitcher will use his index finger on the seam instead of his middle finger. This is for comfort only. The pitcher with a smaller hand may find that such a grip helps his consistency.

Figure 57. Right-handed pitcher slider grip

Figure 58. Left-handed pitcher slider grip

Again, the windup and delivery are identical to the fastball's, as is the arm action. Be sure to get a good finish over the landing leg's knee, with extension. If the finish is lazy, the ball will react poorly and may stay straight.

At the point of release, the wrist will turn just as it does for the curveball. Both right- and left-handers will have a top-to-bottom turn. The fingers need to get out in front of the ball just as with a curveball; the difference is that only the fingertips should rotate down across the front of the ball, whereas in the curveball the whole finger rotates down. Ideally, the fingertips should cut down through the front of the ball in a downward action, putting a bulletlike spin on the ball that is much like the rotation on a thrown football. This is the difference between the curve and the slider: The curve has a rolling action from the fingers, while a slider has more of a cutting action. A good slider looks like

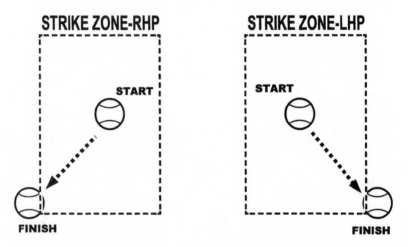

Figure 59. View from mound of slider action

a fastball until it reaches the plate, then gives a short, quick downward motion with just a slight curve break. This will freeze a hitter who is expecting a fastball (see Figure 59).

If a slider is thrown correctly, a red dot will appear out in front. From a batter's perspective (see Figure 60), the dot will appear in a bottom corner of the ball. This appears because all four seams are rotating very tightly. The ball will break in the direction of the corner the dot appears in.

Remember not to break the wrist or turn the ball at any point except the point of release. Concentrate on throwing the ball directly at the catcher's mitt. Let the ball's action carry it down and out of the strike zone.

Cutter

The cutter is thrown just like a fastball—except that at the point of release, the fingers should *not* stay behind the ball. Instead, the wrist should rotate slightly, causing the fingers to come around the side of the ball and giving the ball a spin that is something like a slider's, but with less spin and longer life. The ball will look exactly like a fastball, but instead of running or sinking as a fastball would, it will move in the opposite direction.

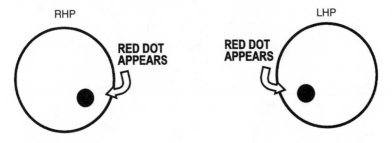

Figure 60. Dot of slider as viewed by hitter

Again, it is important not to release the ball until full extension. Be sure not to let the wrist rotate until the arm reaches a point near full extension. Ideally, there would be no wrist rotation until the ball is just about to be released (see Figures 61–62).

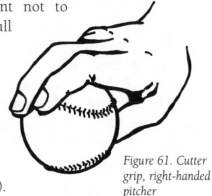

Figure 61. Cutter grip, right-handed pitcher

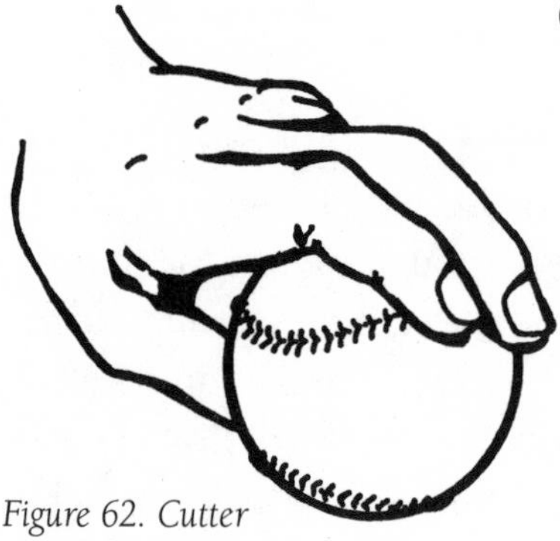

Change-Up

If a young pitcher wants to learn a second pitch, this is the pitch of preference. It is much easier on the arm than a breaking pitch. The idea behind the change-up is to throw the hitter off balance—it looks faster than it really is.

Figure 62. Cutter grip, left-handed pitcher

There are many types of change-up grips, and many types of actions a change can have. I will discuss a few of the most common. Again, the windup, delivery, and arm action are the same as the fastball's. The only difference is the grip—and on certain types of changes the wrist action. Finger pressure may also vary from the normal fastball's.

The most important thing is to remember to use maximum arm speed. This pitch will not be effective if the pitcher slows his arm to any degree. The goal of a good change is to make the hitter believe he is looking at a fastball.

CIRCLE CHANGE

This change gets its name from the grip used, and from the appearance the fingers have on the ball. I recommend holding the ball with the seams, but other grips can be used. Experiment with a variety of grips until one feels good. Still, grip is critical to this pitch.

Hold the ball as if throwing a fastball. Notice that the index and middle fingers are on the ball. Now, replace the index finger with the middle finger, putting it in the exact same spot the index finger was at. Slide the ring finger over to replace the middle finger. The grip now uses the middle and ring fingers instead of the index and middle fingers. The grip on the seams has not changed—just the fingers being used.

Look on the side of the ball; the index finger and thumb have created a backward C for the right-handed pitcher and the letter C for the leftie (see Figures 63–64). The C will vary depending on the size of the pitcher's hands. With large hands

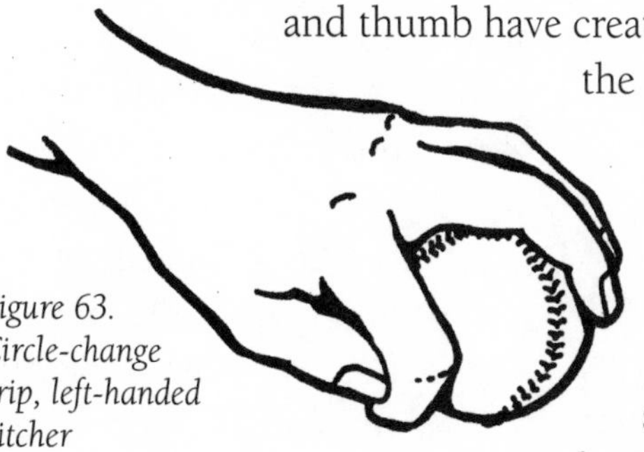

Figure 63. Circle-change grip, left-handed pitcher

the C will become a circle—hence *circle change*. Other than this, however, hand size does not really affect the pitch.

At the point of release, which should be at full extension, the hand will be behind the ball as if it were a fastball, but the grip will slow the ball. Because the index finger is on the side of the ball, it will move more than usual. If the pitch is down in the strike zone, the ball will have a tendency to sink. It is

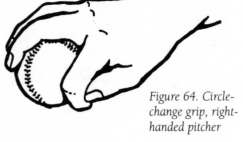

Figure 64. Circle-change grip, right-handed pitcher

important to keep the index finger inside the ball at release and use maximum hand speed to throw the pitch.

THREE-FINGER CHANGE

The three-finger change again uses the regular fastball grip, but this time the ring finger is also involved. It is a good option if a pitcher is not comfortable with the circle-change grip. When the ring finger is on the ball, make sure the ring and index fingers are in contact with the seams (see Figure 65). When throwing this pitch with the across-the-seams grip, be sure the fingertips are on the ball.

The ring finger is used to help reduce the ball's speed. If the pitch is too fast, sometimes placing the ball farther back in the hand can help reduce its speed—this is called *jamming the ball back in the hand*. As with every off-speed pitch, use a good finish and proper arm action.

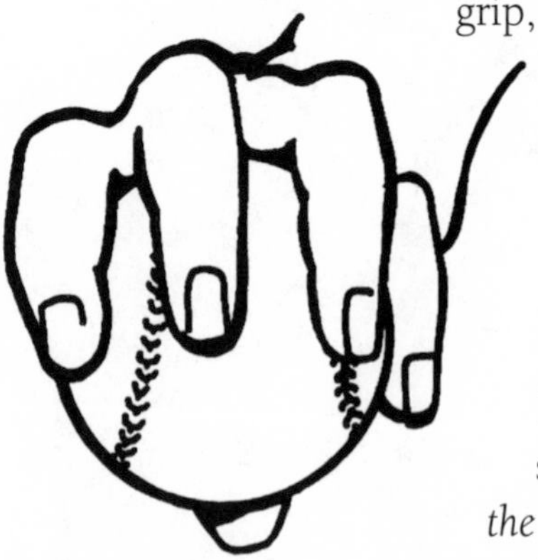

Figure 65. Three-finger change grip

A three-finger change has a running action. On occasion, when it is thrown down in the strike zone, the ball may sink.

JAM CHANGE

This is just what it says: a pitch gripped with all the fingers on the ball, which is placed well back into the palm. It is thrown just like a normal fastball. The ball's placement far back in the hand and the use of all the fingers takes the speed off the ball. There is no trick to this pitch. Get a proper grip and throw it hard. This pitch is very hard to throw and even harder to control.

More than anything else, the change is a means to take speed off the ball. Movement is a plus. Each pitcher should experiment with the grips and find the one that feels most comfortable and is most effective.

Split-Finger Pitch

I do not recommend this pitch for any pitcher under the age of 20. If at all possible, never use this pitch; it is the toughest on your arm.

The split-finger pitch can be held in a variety of positions. The important thing to remember is that the seams should not be part of the grip; the ball should slide out between the index and middle fingers with as little effort as possible. Hold the ball with the index and middle fingers spread as wide as possible (see Figure 66). The proper grip should look and feel as though the ball is wedged between the two fingers. (Pitchers with small hands will struggle with this.) Many pitchers hold the ball with the U portion of the seams upside down. Put the index finger on the outside of one seam and the middle finger on the outside of the other. This will leave the seams inside the split in the fingers (see Figure 66). The fingers at this point are not in contact with any seams.

At release, the ball should come out between the fingers—as opposed to the fastball, where the fingers stay behind the ball. When the ball comes out, it will have less rotation than a fastball, and will tumble downward as it approaches the plate. On occasion the ball may even run like a conventional fastball.

This pitch is intended to look like a fastball without the speed. Unlike a change, if done correctly it will have late, hard movement. The pitcher does not have to worry as much about the feel of the grip or release point; most of this work happens naturally at the release. It is extremely important to keep the elbow above the shoulder or the pitch will not work. A downward angle to the plate is crucial to throwing strikes. Finally, be sure to throw this pitch as hard as possible.

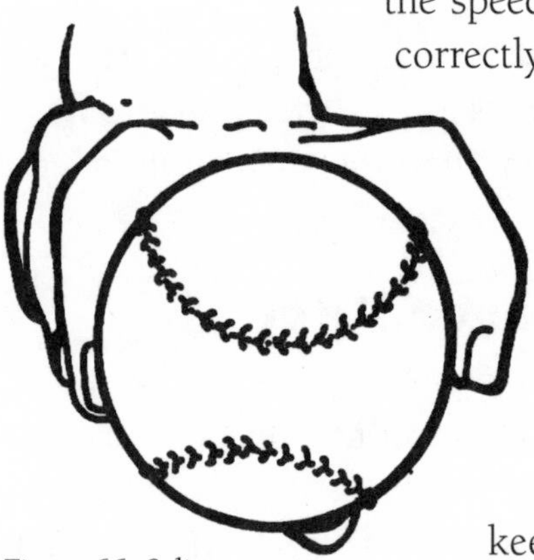

Figure 66. Split-finger grip

Knuckleball

This is often referred to as a trick pitch, because not many pitchers can figure it out and use it effectively. It has nothing to do with speed; the only command needed is to throw it into the strike zone.

The grip can vary depending on the feel. Some pitchers use all fingers, others a two-finger grip (see Figure 67), still others three fingers (see Figure 68). The idea is to find a grip that feels comfortable and will get the ball over the plate.

While all the other pitches rotate at high speed, the knuckleball, if thrown perfectly, will not rotate even once from the release to the catcher's mitt. The wrist should be stiff from the point of taking the ball out of the glove all the way to release; at no point should it bend. The wrist can be on the side of the ball or behind it. Each position gives it a different movement. With the release, the pitcher gives the ball

Figure 67. Two-finger knuckleball grip

an action that is half throw, half push to the plate.

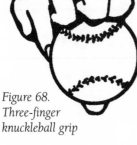

Figure 68. Three-finger knuckleball grip

For the most part, the life on a knuckleball is unpredictable—that is the beauty of the pitch. Remember, there is no emphasis on speed; the speed of the pitch is whatever gives optimum movement and accuracy. Most knuckleball pitchers use this pitch almost exclusively.

Philosophy of the Off-Speed Pitch

Off-speed pitches let a pitcher show the hitter something besides a straight pitch, helping to confuse the hitter's timing and balance. A pitcher should not overuse them, however. It is important to develop and learn to control the fastball. Breaking pitches can then be used to set up the fastball—in other words, the pitcher mixes in breaking stuff to keep a hitter guessing. If he sees one fastball after another, he can begin to adjust to the speed. If he occasionally sees a curve, slider, or change, though, he will not know what to expect, causing him to be less aggressive.

I recommend that a young pitcher not throw breaking pitches too often. Also, use a change more than a curve, slider, or cut fastball. A 14- to 16-year-old pitcher should not throw more than 10 percent breaking pitches in a game.

3

Playing
the Position

Calling the Game

The idea behind calling a game is to throw as few pitches as possible, and throw as many strikes as possible, without giving up runs. The young pitcher does not need to call a game—he is throwing all fastballs. The older pitcher, 13-plus, is now sporting more than a fastball, however, so signals and game calling become important. Major-league pitchers, by the way, throw 70 percent fastballs, even though they may have two to four other pitches.

There are many theories behind calling a game, but the main thing to keep in mind is throwing strikes. Do not lose sight of the fact that there are eight other players in the game, playing defense, who are making plays to help. It is not necessary to strike out every hitter.

Here are some things to remember when calling a game:

- Get ahead in the count.

- Use the fastball as much as possible.

- A well-placed strike on an outside corner is very effective.

- Walks will score a good majority of the time.

- Off-speed pitches are effective when ahead in the count.

- Do not fall in love with off-speed pitches.

- A fastball and a change-up is a good combination.

- Stay out of the middle of the plate when ahead in the count.

- Keep the ball down in the strike zone, no matter what the pitch.

- When the count gets to two balls, two strikes, throw a strike.

- Do not get behind in the count with off-speed pitches.

- Keep track of the batting order. Hitters lower in the order are there for a reason.

- Don't throw the pitch without visualizing the placement.

- Be aggressive.

- Pay attention to where the hitter is in the batter's box. If a hitter is up in the front of the box, he is more susceptible to the fastball because he is closer to the pitcher.

- If the hitter is back in the box, the curveball, slider, or split has more chance to move before he swings.

- If the hitter is standing away from the plate, he is usually diving into the plate. An inside ball is one he will struggle to hit.

- If the hitter is up on the plate, he is struggling with the pitch away and trying to see it better.

- With runners on base, be sure to pay attention to throwing strikes. Very often a pitcher will get so worried about holding the runner that he will start throwing the ball out of the strike zone—and get into more trouble.

- You want to keep the runners close, but before starting the windup and delivery find the catcher's mitt and do not take your eyes from it during the motion. Before the movement starts, head fakes are fine.

- Do not let the umpire affect your pitching strategy. Just continue to throw strikes, even if he continues to miss pitches. Establish the fact that you are a strike thrower and eventually it will pay off. Arguing with the umpire or giving him looks or gestures will not help your cause.

These rules are not foolproof, but they make good starting points.

Signals to and from Catchers

Signals between the pitcher and catcher become important as a pitcher develops. An advanced player will have a variety of pitches—curveball, slider, change-up, knuckleball, cut fastball, sinker, and so on. A catcher needs to know what is coming. He can also signal pitchouts, pickoffs, or intentional walks.

A catcher signals a fastball by putting one finger down. The curveball is signaled by two fingers, the slider by three, a change-up by four (see Figure 69).

A *pickoff* is signaled by the hitchhike sign. This play does not have to be called by the catcher; a pitcher can pick off on his own.

A *pitchout* is signaled by a closed fist. A pitchout is when the pitcher throws the ball chest-high in the unoccupied batter's box. He should go through the delivery just as if he were

Figure 69. Catcher's signals—two fingers indicates curveball

throwing a strike, and the catcher should stay in the squat as long as possible. This is designed to give the catcher an advantage trying to throw to second on an attempted steal.

An *intentional walk* is signaled by the catcher standing straight up and sticking his throwing hand into the unoccupied batter's box. This play prevents a hitter from getting a chance to get a hit or help score a run by making contact with the pitched ball.

A catcher may give a location signal after the pitch is called. He does this by lightly tapping the inside of his leg on the side he wants the pitch to be thrown. He may also give a low or high signal by moving his fingers in the desired direction after the pitch is called. He might also tap his chest after the call, meaning "throw the ball up in the strike zone."

A pitcher can change the signal if he is not satisfied with the call. There are a number of ways he can do this:

• Shaking his head no.

• Wiping his leg or shirt with his glove.

• Not shaking his head until the proper call is made.

When a runner is on second, a catcher and pitcher might use a separate set of signs, because otherwise the runner can signal the hitter what to expect. For example, the catcher could give a sequence of signals, one of which is the call. By prearrangement, both catcher and pitcher know that the *second* signal is the call. In this case the catcher might put down one finger, two fingers, and two fingers. This indicates a curveball, because the second signal was a two.

Even more complicated signals are sometimes developed—for instance, first signal after an indicator. Just for fun, let's try a few. The indicator could be fastball. The catcher puts down two fingers, two fingers, one finger, and then three fingers. This is a slider: The first signal after the fastball was the slider.

The pitcher can also change the call from the catcher by means of a signal. Let's say the pitcher can add or subtract a pitch by rubbing his leg for subtracting, or rubbing his chest for adding. Let's further say that the indicator is second signal after the curveball. The catcher signals 1–3–2–1–2; the pitcher rubs his leg. The pitch is a fastball. The second signal after the curveball was a curveball, but the pitcher rubbed his leg, meaning "subtract one."

Clearly, a runner is better off not trying to relay calls to the hitter. He most often will be of no help.

Stretch

The stretch is a special starting point that a pitcher uses with runners on base. It is for advanced players: At the Little League level it is not necessary, because rules prohibit stealing until the ball crosses the plate. Still, the stretch is a very handy way to teach young players the mechanics of delivery without spending extra time running through the windup portion of the pitching motion. Also, at higher levels of the game pitchers need to keep runners close to the base to prevent steals.

The stretch starts with the pitcher standing on the mound with his body facing to the side, rather than directly at the catcher. A right-handed pitcher will be facing third base; a left-hander will face first base. The feet should be positioned together, with the back foot in the hole in front of the rubber (see Figure 70). This is the same position a pitcher reaches after the rocker-step portion of the windup. From this point, the pitcher lifts his front leg to the leg-kick position, attempting to find the balance point. The rest of the delivery is the same as in the earlier discussion of the windup and delivery.

Using this delivery instead of a windup will allow the young pitcher to better find his balance point and develop proper direction. As soon as the young pitcher masters these mechanics, move him back into the windup.

Figure 70. Getting signal at beginning of stretch

Slide Step

The slide step is used out of the stretch mainly to hold runners close to the base, and also to give the catcher a chance to throw base stealers out. The slide step is much like the conventional stretch, except the leg kick is eliminated or greatly reduced (see Figure 71). This is not hard to do, but with the reduction or elimination of the leg kick pitchers will find it hard to get to the loaded portion in time for a proper throw to the plate (see Figure 71). It may help to shorten the arm arc when in the slide step. If a pitcher is still having trouble getting to the load, breaking the hands at the first move to the plate will allow the arc to be completed in time to throw correctly. Be sure to finish the

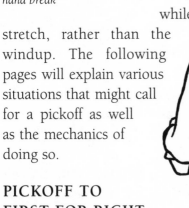

Figure 71. Slide step hand break

pitch, no matter what approach is used (see Figure 72).

If the slide step causes problems with the pitch's control, velocity, or life, use the conventional stretch. The idea is to get the hitter out. This is the pitcher's primary job.

Pickoffs

A pickoff is a move designed to catch a runner off base, forcing him out. Pitchers use it most commonly while in the stretch, rather than the windup. The following pages will explain various situations that might call for a pickoff as well as the mechanics of doing so.

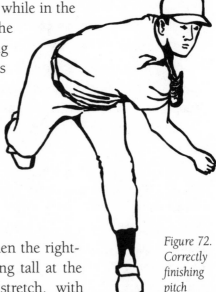

Figure 72. Correctly finishing pitch

PICKOFF TO FIRST FOR RIGHT-HANDERS

This move starts when the right-handed pitcher is standing tall at the very beginning of the stretch, with both feet together and the back foot in the hole in contact with the rubber (see Figure 70). His first act is to glance over his left shoulder to see where the runner is in relation to the base, and to make sure the position player is covering the bag so that when he throws the ball over, someone is there to catch it.

Do not move the legs in any way. If any part of the body moves—other than the head—it is illegal.

When it is decided that a throw to first is necessary, the pitcher should return his focus to the catcher's mitt as if he were going to deliver to the plate. Then he quickly picks up his right foot, moves it about 6 inches toward third base, and plants it back on the ground while having rotated it counterclockwise so its toes are now pointed at home plate. At this same time the hands should break apart, preparing to deliver the ball to first (see Figure 73). When the foot returns to the ground, the arm should be in position to deliver the ball to first. Quickly make a short stride to first with the front foot, then make an accurate knee-high throw that reaches the first baseman on the side of the bag where the runner is returning.

Here are some things to remember:

- Try to shorten the arm action to deliver the ball more quickly (see Figure 74).

- Remember not to move the body before a pickoff starts, especially not the shoulders or legs.

- Look over toward first before attempting this move to make sure someone will be there to catch the ball.

- Unlike the throw to home, it is not mandatory to maintain contact with the rubber during the throw.

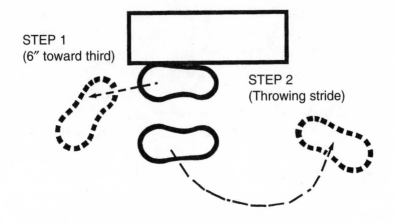

STEP 1
(6" toward third)

STEP 2
(Throwing stride)

Figure 73. Footwork for pickoff to first, right-handed pitcher

- The front foot must stride in the direction of the throw.

- Try to grip the ball across the seams to eliminate any added movement on the throw.

- It is illegal to fake a throw after starting the pickoff move.

- If the pitcher steps off the back of the rubber with his back foot before the start of the delivery or pickoff move, a fake throw to first is perfectly legal. Be sure that contact with the rubber is broken. Also, with the foot off the rubber a pitch to the plate cannot be attempted.

PICKOFF TO FIRST FOR LEFT-HANDERS

This pickoff is totally different than the right-hander's (see Figure 75), because the leftie is facing the runner at first where the right-hander has his back to the runner. First, the left-handed pitcher should decide if the runner is far enough off the base to require a throw. If so, the next move is to start the delivery to the plate. The pitcher first starts to lift his leg (see Figure 76) as if a throw to home were coming. At any point in this leg kick, he can throw to first by striding toward that base (see Figure 77), rather than home,

Figure 74. Hand break and stride to first

and delivering the ball with a knee-high throw on the side of the bag where the runner is returning.

This pickoff move can be varied. The pitcher might throw over at different points in his leg kick, or even before the leg kick begins. He can also use his head—sometimes looking over and throwing and sometimes looking toward home then throwing over to first. In the latter

Figure 75. Stretch for left-handed pitcher, facing first base

case, be sure to turn the head and pick up your target *before* delivering the ball to first to aid in accuracy (see Figure 78).

Here are some things to remember:

- The grip should be across the seams.

- You must stride toward the base you are throwing at.

- The body must not move prior to starting the delivery—no leg movement, no shoulder movement.

Figure 76. Lift front foot, can go to first or home

- If an attempt is made to throw to first, the throw must be completed—fakes are illegal.

- Try to keep this move to first as close to looking like a throw to home as possible, helping to disguise it.

Figure 77. Top of leg kick, still can go home or first

- The stride to first cannot create an angle over 45 degrees between first and home (see Figure 79).

- If the pitcher steps off the back of the rubber with his back foot before the start of

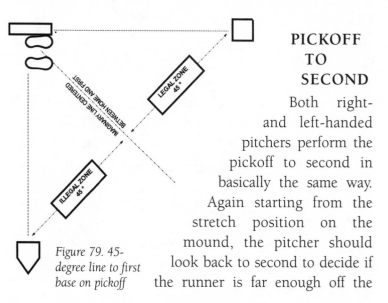

Figure 78. Keep eyes on target

the delivery or pickoff move, a fake throw to first is perfectly legal. Be sure that contact with the rubber is broken. Also, with the foot off the rubber a pitch to the plate cannot be attempted.

Figure 79. 45-degree line to first base on pickoff

PICKOFF TO SECOND

Both right- and left-handed pitchers perform the pickoff to second in basically the same way. Again starting from the stretch position on the mound, the pitcher should look back to second to decide if the runner is far enough off the base to attempt a pickoff. If he is, the pitcher should also know who is covering second base. Will it be the second baseman or shortstop? This is made clear by use of signals. The first move is to step off the rubber (see Figure 80) by picking up the back foot and moving it approximately 6 inches back in the direction of second base. When the foot

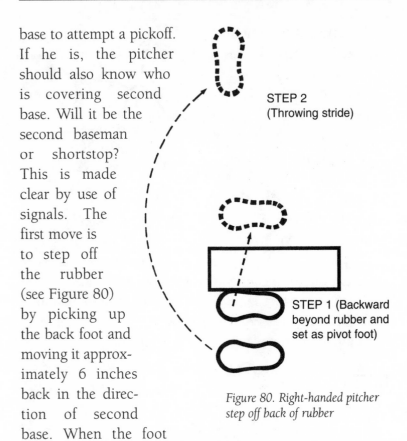

STEP 2
(Throwing stride)

STEP 1 (Backward beyond rubber and set as pivot foot)

Figure 80. Right-handed pitcher step off back of rubber

returns to the ground behind the rubber, rotate the body around in the direction of the glove shoulder. If a right-handed pitcher is making the move, he needs to rotate counterclockwise (see Figure 81); a left-hander rotates clockwise. Make the rotation quick and short to eliminate precious time. Be sure to find the person covering second base as soon as possible, then make an accurate throw waist-high on the side of the bag the runner is returning to. A low throw is hard for a position player to catch while racing toward the base.

Remember, a throw is not required in this situation, because the foot is not in contact with the rubber.

Here are some things to remember:

• Pick up the person receiving the throw as soon as possible.

• Rotate toward the glove shoulder.

• Try to eliminate any unnecessary body movements.

• Shorten the arm action to speed the throwing time.

• Make an accurate belt-high throw.

• A fake throw is legal.

Figure 81. Rotate counterclockwise to second base

There are other ways to execute a pickoff to second. A second type is a spin move. A right-handed pitcher should step with his back foot to the same position it was in for a throw to first. Now rotate the body counterclockwise and throw to second with a short, quick arm action (see Figure 82). A left-handed pitcher should step with his back foot to the point on the mound where his front foot is presently planted. As he moves his back foot, his front foot should

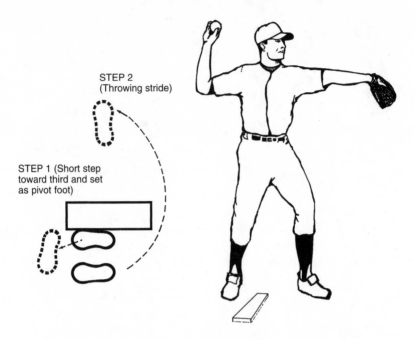

STEP 2
(Throwing stride)

STEP 1 (Short step
toward third and set
as pivot foot)

Figure 82. Spin move to second base, right-handed pitcher

move toward second base and become the stride foot. The body should move clockwise.

This is identical to the first move to second, except the back foot does not step back; here it steps forward. Again, be sure to use a quick shorter arc to reduce throwing time. Fake throws are legal, because the pitcher has broken contact with the rubber.

A third move to second is the inside move, performed in the same way by both right- and left-handers. In the stretch, lift the leg as if throwing a pitch to home. At the top of the leg kick, rotate the body counterclockwise for the left-handed pitcher, or clockwise for the right-hander.

Return the front foot to the ground behind the rubber and throw to second. Again, a fake throw is allowed. This move often will catch a runner who is stealing third on the pitcher's first movement in the stretch (see Figure 83).

Figure 83. Inside move to second base, right-handed pitcher

PICKOFF-TO-SECOND SIGNALS

Many different signs can be used for the pickoff to second; the main thing is that both the pitcher and the fielder know a throw will be made. When the pitcher gets to the set position, he needs to look back to second. At this point the signal is made. What follow are some basic signs.

If the shortstop or second baseman wants the throw to be made, he will sprint to the base with his glove open and arm stretched to the base. This will tell the pitcher to throw to the base. He might use an inside or spin move in this situation.

Another type of signal is the timing play. When the pitcher or infielder wants to put on this play, he needs to signal prior to the pitcher stepping onto the mound. The infielder needs to get the pitcher's attention and give a signal. Simply taking off the glove will do. When the pitcher sees this signal, he in turn will pick at his shirt or take off his hat—whatever has been agreed upon. Now the pickoff is on. The spin move is used. When the pitcher gets to the set position (see Figure 75), he counts 1001, 1002, 1003. On 1002 the infielder runs to second base to receive the throw; on 1003 the pitcher spins and throws belt-high to the base. The one-second difference in starting time will allow the fielder to be in position for the throw.

PICKOFF TO THIRD

I recommend using this pickoff as seldom as possible. A pickoff to third is rarely successful, and if executed incorrectly, the runner will easily score. That said, here is how to perform the pickoff to third. If in the stretch, a right-handed pitcher lifts his leg as if a pitch to home is coming. At the top of the kick, he strides toward third and throws. Be sure to step toward third and not home, for the step to home is illegal if attempting the pickoff (see Figure 84). A left-handed pitcher picks up his back foot, moves it behind the rubber, and returns it to the ground. Rotate the body toward third and attempt the throw.

A fake throw is perfectly legal. Be sure to use a short arc when throwing, to save time (see Figure 85).

Defense on the Mound

As well as throwing strikes and keeping hitters from reaching base, a pitcher has to field his position. As a rule of thumb, it is more important for the pitcher to throw strikes with the best control, velocity, and movement possible. After he has accomplished this, he must

Figure 84. Top of kick

do his very best to field balls hit back at him, cover bases that the other defensive players are unable to, and back up bases where plays are being made in case of an errant throw.

FIELDING A GROUND BALL

After the release of the ball and the finish have been completed (see Figure 86), it is time to field a ball hit back to the pitcher. The first thing the pitcher needs to do is

Figure 85. Step-back pickoff to third, left-handed pitcher

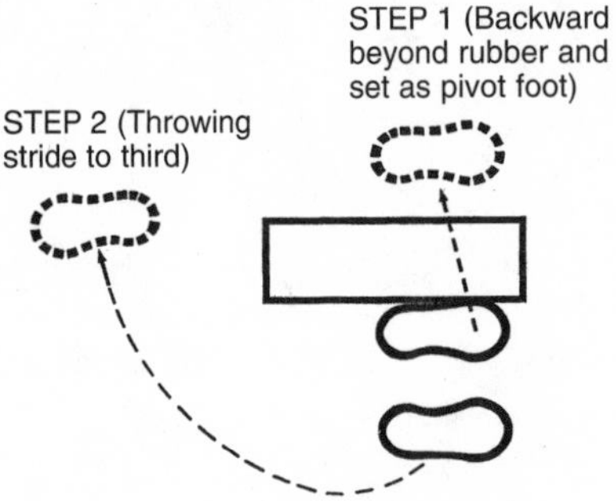

STEP 1 (Backward beyond rubber and set as pivot foot)

STEP 2 (Throwing stride to third)

Figure 86. Finish motion

regain his balance (see Figure 87), then recover sight of the ball. If the ball is in fielding distance, a pitcher should run to it—under control. He should try to meet the ball at a point where he can position himself to make an easy pivot and throw to first (see Figures 88–90). A *pivot* is a con-

Figure 87. Regain balance, find ball

trolled turn in the direction of the base to be thrown to. Very often a pitcher will run full speed in the direction of the ball and pick it up—only to spin out of control and throw the ball right past the player covering the base. A pitcher should always stride in the direction he is attempting to throw the ball before making a throw. When running to pick the ball up, it is also important to run on the balls of the feet, not flat-footed; this gives better control.

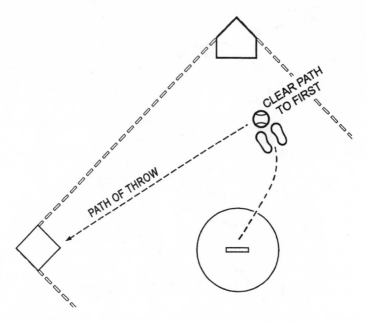

Figure 88. Correct angle to field

Try to catch the ball out in front of your body, much like an infielder (see Figure 91). Catching the ball underneath the body will most likely result in fumbling, because the eyes lose sight of the ball for a split second. It is also important to get a good grip on the ball. If possible, grip it across the seams to cut down on its movement when thrown.

If the ball is wet, using a third finger to throw is very helpful. This should be the ring finger. Try not to throw the ball with a hump in it, meaning too softly. It is hard to control a soft throw. It also gives the runner time to make the play close, which puts pressure on the fielder catching the

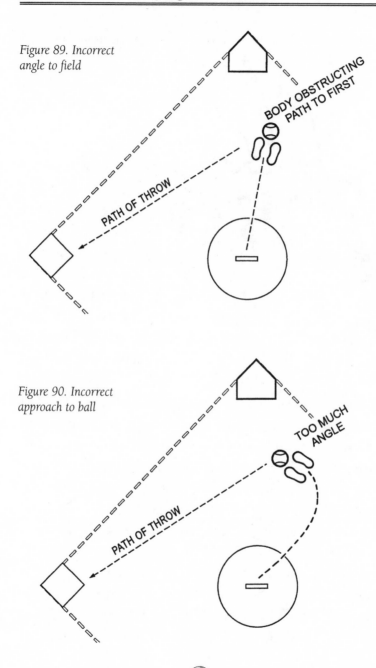

Figure 89. Incorrect angle to field

Figure 90. Incorrect approach to ball

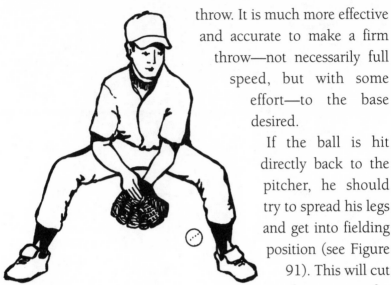

Figure 91. Spread legs and field ball in front of body

throw. It is much more effective and accurate to make a firm throw—not necessarily full speed, but with some effort—to the base desired.

If the ball is hit directly back to the pitcher, he should try to spread his legs and get into fielding position (see Figure 91). This will cut down on the chance of stumbling while fielding. For the most part, a pitcher is a goalie. Most of the time he does not have time to do anything but knock the ball down. The main thing is to stop it and try to make an accurate throw. If a poor grip or balance makes an errant throw likely, do not attempt it. It is better to keep the runner to first base than to make an error and allow him to get extra bases.

If the ball being fielded has stopped—for instance, a bunt or swinging bunt—pick it up with your bare hand. This play is much easier without the glove. Fielding a stopped ball with the glove increases the chances of fumbling the ball while picking it up. And even if it is picked up, transferring the ball to the bare hand is an additional

opportuni-
ty to juggle
the ball. Use
a bare hand.

PLAYS TO FIRST

Anytime a play to
first is being made,
try to step in the
direction of the
base (see
Figure 92)
and then
throw. Do
not attempt

Figure 92. Step and throw

the throw flat-footed—that is, with both feet stationary
and no stride in the direction of the throw (see Figure 93).

If the throw to first is very short, an underhand throw
is acceptable. Again, be sure to step and then underhand the
ball. Another important thing to remember, on the underhand throw, is to make the ball visible quickly. Separate the
glove and the throwing hand with the ball in it as soon as
possible, giving the player receiving the ball every opportunity to see the ball early. If the pitcher fields the ball
extremely close to the base, it is also fine to simply touch
the base, without use of a throw. Be sure to communicate
with the fielders to allow them to get out of the way. "I'll
take it" or "I got it" are typical calls in this situation.

A pitcher may need to cover first base himself if the ball is hit to the first baseman or just to the second-base side of him. Here, the first baseman has traveled too far to return to the base, so it is the pitcher's responsibility to get to first and receive the throw (see Figure 94). As the ball is hit to the pitcher's left, he should run to the restraining line at full speed. At the line, he turns and runs parallel to the line as if he were a base runner. He then looks to receive the ball from the fielder while on the run, and touches the base on the inside edge to avoid

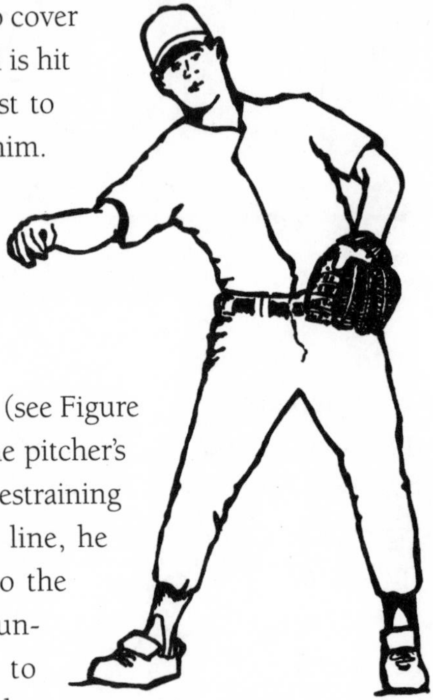

Figure 93. No step, poor throwing angle

tripping over the runner. After touching, he turns and runs inside the baseline in fair territory, again so as not to interfere with the runner crossing the base. As soon as possible, turn and prepare to make a throw on another runner, if needed.

If you are able to get to the base before a throw is made, stop at the base and set up as if you were a first baseman. Do not attempt to pace your run to catch the ball at the same time you reach the base—it is very diffi-

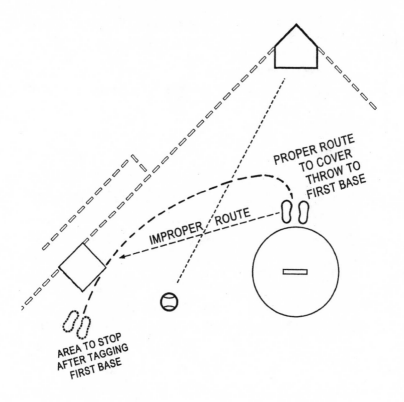

Figure 94. Angles to use covering first base

cult to catch the ball and tag the base at the same time. While running to the base, try to use two hands to catch the thrown ball to reduce any chance of mishandling it. And finally, a small point: If possible, try to touch the base with the right foot. If not, just be sure to touch the base and get the out.

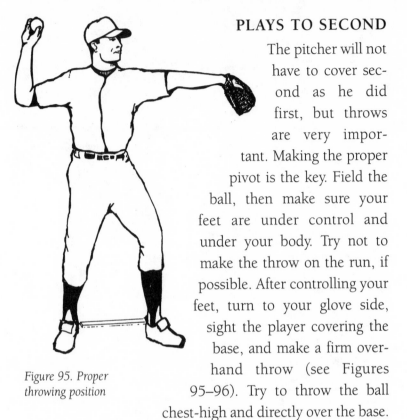

Figure 95. Proper throwing position

PLAYS TO SECOND

The pitcher will not have to cover second as he did first, but throws are very important. Making the proper pivot is the key. Field the ball, then make sure your feet are under control and under your body. Try not to make the throw on the run, if possible. After controlling your feet, turn to your glove side, sight the player covering the base, and make a firm overhand throw (see Figures 95–96). Try to throw the ball chest-high and directly over the base. Leading the defensive player might seem to be a good ploy, but more often than not this throw is mishandled.

PLAYS TO THIRD

It is extremely important to make an accurate throw to third base; a poor one will result in a run. The throw to third is executed just like the throw to second. Be sure to step and throw with a good grip on the ball. Make the throw chest-high. Do not rush. Proper footwork is a must.

THROWS TO HOME

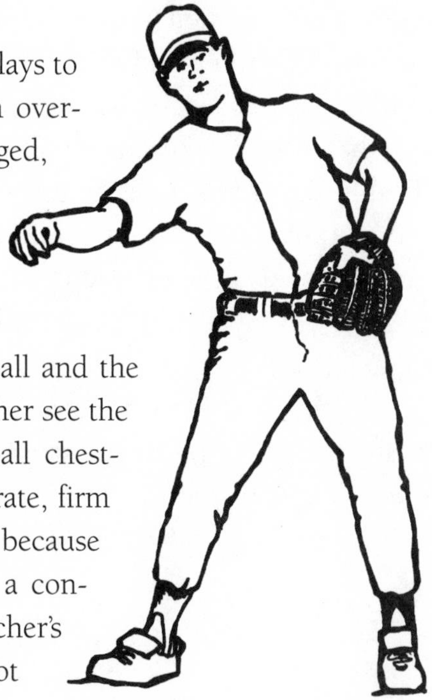

There are very few plays to home, but a step and an overhand throw are encouraged, if possible. At times, it is necessary to underhand a throw to the plate. In this instance, be sure to separate the ball and the glove early to let the catcher see the ball. Again, throw the ball chest-high and firmly. An accurate, firm throw is also important because the catcher is using not a conventional glove but a catcher's mitt. A soft throw will not stay in this mitt, because it does not fold the way a fielder's glove does.

Figure 96. Incorrect throwing angle

BACKING UP THE BASES

There isn't much to know about backing up the bases. The most important thing is to hustle to the spot. Remember, you can never get to a position too early. Also, stay far enough away from the play to see the throw and the base thrown to. Getting too close to the action will allow the ball to get by both you and the baseman. Try to stay far enough back to cut off the ball before it goes out of play.

More important is knowing when to back up. When a runner is on first and the ball is hit for what could be a double, the pitcher should back up third, because the play may be to third. Run quickly to the deepest point behind third in direct line with the throw being made. Be sure to set up in play and not out of bounds. If a runner is on second and the ball is hit deep enough to advance him, the backup third position is also taken by the pitcher (see Figure 97).

With a runner trying to score, for any reason, on a hit or fly ball, try to get to the backstop behind the plate in a direct line with the throw. If you set up too close to the

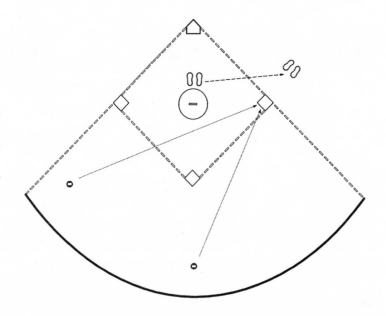

Figure 97. Backing up third base

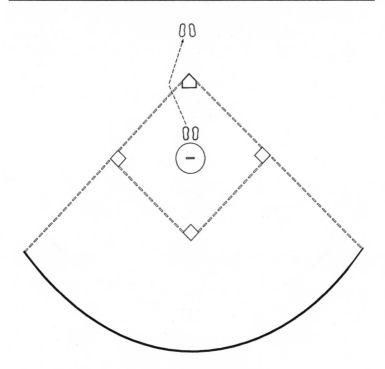

Figure 98. Backing up home

catcher, you might get in his way—or the throw might go over his head and yours (see Figure 98).

If for some reason a play could come to either third or home, hustle to a spot halfway between home and third as close to out of play as possible. Watch the play develop and run to the most likely spot (see Figure 99).

Occasionally a runner at first will be trying to return to the base while a throw is being made to first. In this case, run to the deepest point behind first that is still in bounds and line yourself up with the incoming throw. Keep in mind

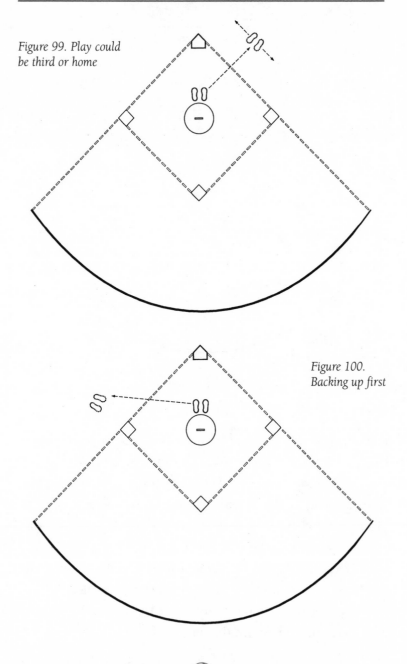

Figure 99. Play could be third or home

Figure 100. Backing up first

that if there is no play at the plate, the catcher will also be backing up here (see Figure 100).

Another situation in which a pitcher can back up and be of service is a base hit with nobody on base and the throw coming to second (see Figure 101). Once in a while the ball will be overthrown, and your backup can stop the runner rounding first from advancing to second. Position yourself halfway between first and second, lined up with the throw. Be sure to not get in the runner's way. This could cause interference. If the throw is from right field, halfway between second and third is the proper spot (see Figure 102). Remember, do not get in the way of the other fielders or runners while backing up. Just do your best to be in position and help if needed.

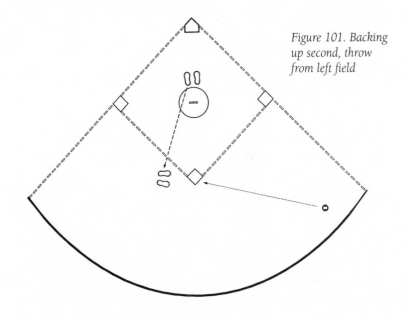

Figure 101. Backing up second, throw from left field

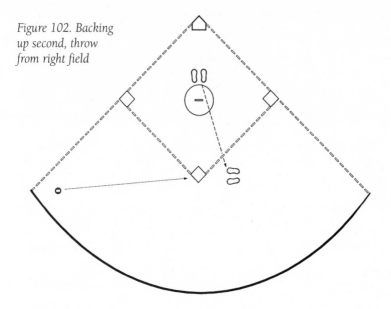

Figure 102. Backing up second, throw from right field

RUNDOWNS

When a runner gets trapped between two bases, the defense may try to tag him out with a *rundown*. What are the pitcher's responsibilities in this situation?

If a runner on first is being run down between first and second, line up behind the first baseman, forming a line with him and the catcher. When the defensive player comes toward first, chasing the runner back, give a target and be prepared to catch the ball (see Figure 103). Position yourself one to two steps in front of the base to keep the runner from returning without being tagged. If he changes direction and runs to second with the ball in your possession, run hard at the runner—under control—with the ball over your head (see Figure 104). Deliver the ball to the player covering second as soon as the runner is at full speed. After throwing the ball to your teammate, get out of the way by getting in the line behind the players at second (see Figure 105).

Rundowns between second and third follow the same procedure, but start by getting in line at third base

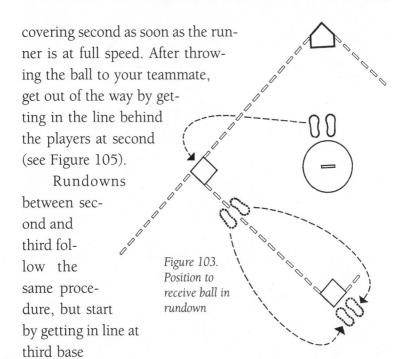

Figure 103.
Position to
receive ball in
rundown

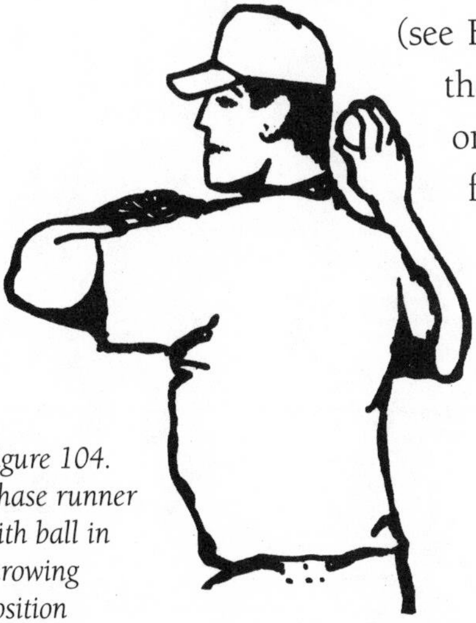

Figure 104.
Chase runner
with ball in
throwing
position

(see Figure 106). After throwing the ball to the player at second, get in line behind the formed line at second. With the rundown between third and home, again use the same procedure, but start at home plate behind the catcher (see Figure 107); after the throw to third, fall in line at third.

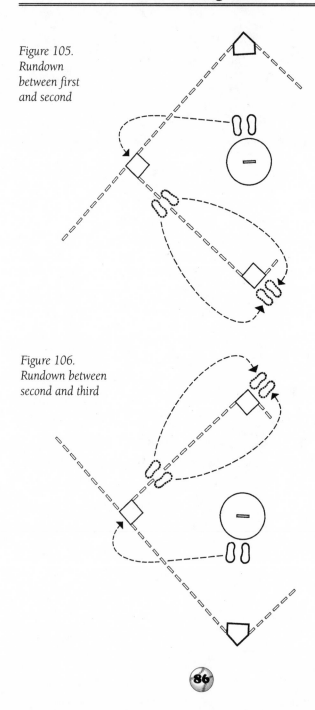

*Figure 105.
Rundown
between first
and second*

*Figure 106.
Rundown between
second and third*

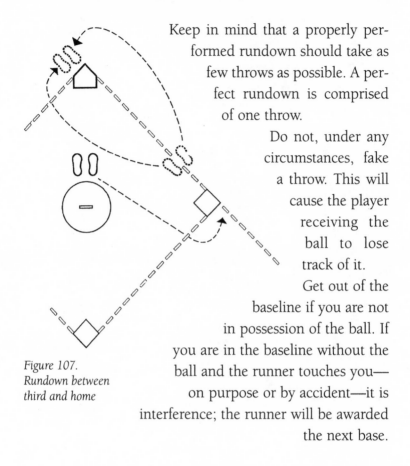

Figure 107.
Rundown between
third and home

Keep in mind that a properly performed rundown should take as few throws as possible. A perfect rundown is comprised of one throw.

Do not, under any circumstances, fake a throw. This will cause the player receiving the ball to lose track of it.

Get out of the baseline if you are not in possession of the ball. If you are in the baseline without the ball and the runner touches you—on purpose or by accident—it is interference; the runner will be awarded the next base.

4

Practice and Conditioning

Practice Drills for Common Problems

The following pages list both common problems and a helpful drill or two to solve them. Keep in mind that some problems are harder to fix than others. Most need to be addressed when the pitcher is throwing half speed or less. Working on problems when the pitcher is throwing full speed makes correction almost impossible.

- **Late-breaking hands:** Practice the windup and break your hands from the glove as your knee lifts to the leg kick. Or stand in front of a mirror and watch your hands break from your glove as if the knee were causing the action to happen.

- **Rocker step or pivot step:** Use a mound with a functional rubber or a flat piece of scrap wood. Address the mound as if you were looking for the target. Practice the small step straight back. The idea is to keep your head from moving in any direction.

- **Understriding:** To correct understriding, at the top of the kick as you are ready to stride to the plate, point the toe of your leg-kick foot slightly up in the air. This will cause the foot to travel a few inches farther before you return to the balls of your feet at landing. Adjust the toe point until the ball of the foot lands correctly (see Figure 108).

- **Leg kick too small:** Perform the windup in the mirror or have the coach view your windup and delivery. When your landing foot hits the ground, your hand should be at the loaded position. If your hand has not yet reached the loaded position, your kick is too small. Adjust the kick until you achieve the loaded position at the point of landing.

- **Leg kick too high:** If you reach the loaded position before your stride foot lands on the ground, do not lift your leg as high in the leg kick. Continue reducing the kick until your arm is loaded at landing.

- **Overstriding:** Correct over-striding by pointing the toe of your leg-kick foot down to the ground during the kick. Adjust the pointing of the foot according to how much the stride needs to be short-ened. Having the toe down will allow the foot to land earlier (see Figure 109).

Figure 108. Toe up in kick

- **Incorrect glove position:** Not getting the glove out in front or having the glove in the wrong position can both be worked on with the same drill. Get down on one knee. A right-handed pitcher should be on his right knee, and vice versa. Put the other foot out in front of your body, at a comfortable point. Now practice throwing to another player or to a wall, concentrating on proper arm mechanics—glove hand extended to the tar-

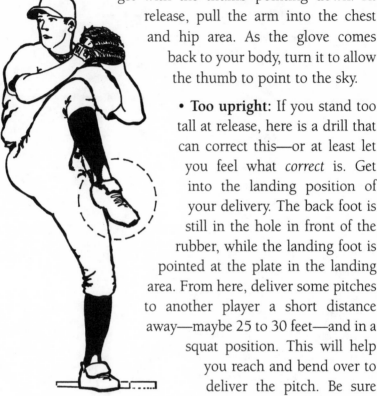

Figure 109. Toe down in kick

get with the thumb pointing down. At release, pull the arm into the chest and hip area. As the glove comes back to your body, turn it to allow the thumb to point to the sky.

• **Too upright:** If you stand too tall at release, here is a drill that can correct this—or at least let you feel what *correct* is. Get into the landing position of your delivery. The back foot is still in the hole in front of the rubber, while the landing foot is pointed at the plate in the landing area. From here, deliver some pitches to another player a short distance away—maybe 25 to 30 feet—and in a squat position. This will help you reach and bend over to deliver the pitch. Be sure not to stride while throwing (see Figure 110).

• **Collapse out front:** Use the drill explained under "Too upright," but shorten your stride until your body stays more upright in the delivery. The drill found under "Overstriding" may also be helpful.

• **Direction problems:** The first thing to determine is what is causing this trouble. One way to do so is to start at the top of the kick with your hands broken. Stop and assume a statue position. If you lose your balance, this is the problem. Once you achieve balance, continue the delivery with a direct foot move from the top of the kick to the landing area. Then check your rocker step, and make sure the back knee is breaking in the proper angle to the plate.

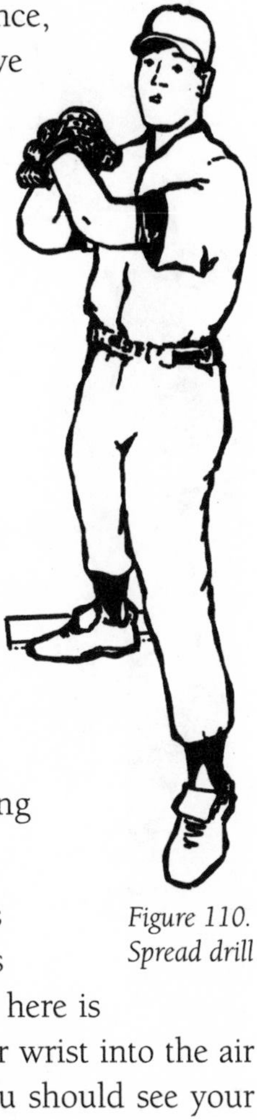

- **Arm-action trouble:** This is very hard to correct. Start a routine of playing toss with someone, at a short distance, concentrating on the mechanics of the arm action discussed earlier. A long throw is no help; a short, easy-to-reach distance is best. Have the other player give a target. Work on developing your arc.

*Figure 110.
Spread drill*

- **Not behind the ball:** This problem is usually caused because the wrist turns prior to release. A drill that is effective here is to stand still and flip the ball with your wrist into the air over your head a number of times. You should see your incorrect release and be able to practice a correct one without wearing out your arm delivering pitches.

- **Arched back** (see Figure 111): Keep in mind that an overhand pitcher will have some arch naturally. At the top of the kick, the balance point, be sure the shoulders and hips are directly on top of each other. Do not let the shoulders stray from the upright position.

- **Front shoulder lift** (see Figure 112): At the top of the kick, be sure the front shoulder is even with the back shoulder. It is also acceptable to have the front shoulder slightly lower than the back shoulder.

- **Upper body too forward:** Go through the windup. At the top of the kick, stop. If you cannot stop and instead fall forward, this is a problem of both balance and direction. Continue trying the windup until you can stop at the top of the kick with no trouble.

Figure 111.
Arched back

- **Poor rotation of hips:** Not pulling the glove into the body at release, and failing to extend the glove have the same cause. Get on one knee, as described under "Incorrect glove position," and throw with a partner, concentrating on glove work. Another drill is to get on the mound in the delivery position—back foot in the hole in front of the rubber, landing foot in the landing position—and work on pulling in the glove at the point of throwing. Sometimes the poor hip rotation stems from throwing across the body.

• **Arm angle inconsistent:** Throw to a catcher. If the inconsistent arm angle is too low, have the catcher stay 65 feet away; you will have to get your arm up to reach the catcher. If the angle is too high, put the catcher 35 feet away. You will drop the angle to throw a strike at a short distance. Continue to move in the direction of the plate until it is comfortable to throw from the correct arm angle.

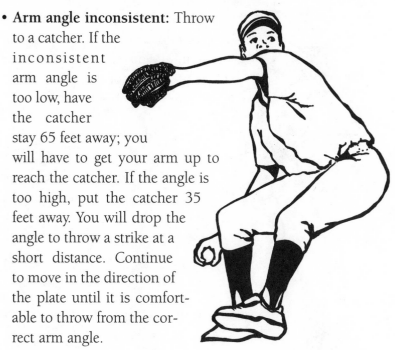

Figure 112. Front shoulder lift

• **Underkick** (see Figure 113): At the top of the leg kick, your foot should be at its farthest point from the body. If the foot is close to or under the body, extend your knee out even with your waist with your foot directly under your knee. This will allow you to use your hip during delivery.

• **Jumping:** This is the act of pushing up off the rubber instead of at the catcher. Get to the balanced position and bend your back knee slightly, then push in the direction of the plate instead of up out of the balance point.

• **Poor back-leg use:** At the balance point, the back knee needs to break slightly toward the catcher. Otherwise, you

95

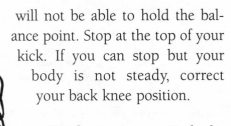

will not be able to hold the balance point. Stop at the top of your kick. If you can stop but your body is not steady, correct your back knee position.

• **Head movement:** Tuck the chin into the front shoulder until the landing foot heads for the plate; then continue the motion as usual. At this point, it is too late for the head to be a problem. Try to keep your head steady from start to finish.

Figure 113. Under-kicking, leg too far under body

• **Too open or too closed:** These can be corrected with the same drill. Start by drawing a line in the dirt on the mound from the spot you start the address and extend it down the mound in the exact direction of the plate. Now throw a few pitches. You should land on the line or very close. Standing with your back foot in the hole and your landing foot on the line, throw a few pitches to feel the correct landing area.

• **Heel landing:** To correct this, shorten the stride with the toe-down method. At the top of the kick, point the toe slightly down, allowing the foot to land at a shorter position and either flat or up on the ball of the foot.

- **Rolling over** (see Figure 114): If you are rolling over on your front ankle regularly, balance is the problem. Start by shortening your stride. If this does not work, get to your balance point, then stride directly to the catcher to stop the problem.

- **Hurry windup:** Try to get a longer leg kick. This will slow the delivery, because the body will have to wait for the foot to hit the ground. If this does not work, a bigger arc in the arm action should slow the release time.

Figure 114. Rolling over on the landing foot

- **Leg sweep:** This happens when the leg-kick-to-landing action is not direct; you instead swing your leg from the top of the kick to the landing area. The drill to help stop this is to put a 5-gallon bucket or cone in the area the foot should not travel. As you become more direct, continue to move the cone or bucket until you reach the desired directness (see Figure 115).

- **Windup too slow:** Shorten the leg kick and or shorten the arc on the arm action. This will force the ball to be thrown more quickly.

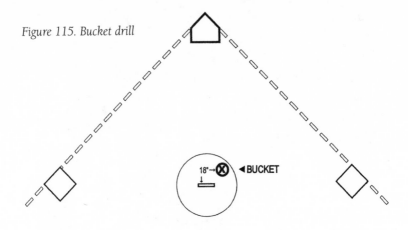

Figure 115. Bucket drill

- **Long arm action:** Start in the post position. You do not have a ball, but a partner does. The partner needs to hand the ball to you in the post position, at your back hip, as you start the motion to the plate. The idea is to stop you from arcing the ball well below your waist or too far from your body. This drill will also help the pitcher whose arc is too short (see Figure 116).

- **Short arm action:** The drill discussed under "Long arm action" will help. The only difference is that here the partner holds the

Figure 116. Partner drill to correct arc problems

ball slightly below the waist to force you to extend your arc (see Figure 116).

- **Upper-body rotation trouble:** Stand as if to field a ground ball with your feet and shoulders facing the catcher (see Figure 117). The feet should be shoulder-width apart. Without striding, rotate your hips and perform the arm action delivering the ball to the catcher. This will give you the feeling of using the hips correctly. *Be sure you are very loose before attempting to throw from the flat-footed position,* as described here.

- **Dead front side:** Start with the glove fully extended to a partner, who should be 45 to 50 feet away. Concentrate on pulling the glove in as you throw the ball. This can be done with any type of pitch. Try to have the arm action run through the whole arc (see Figures 118–119).

- **Slow arm:** Stand with a partner toss-and-catch distance apart. As you get loose, have the partner slowly move farther away. Continue to move apart until you can no longer reach the partner. At this point, throw 20 to 25 pitches. Repeat once a week until corrected.

- **Not over front leg:** Place a chair on flat ground and stand in front of it (see Figure 120). Place your land-

Figure 117. Straddle drill

ing foot, toes in, on the ground in the landing area. Place your back foot on the chair. Now throw to the plate. You should feel extension out front. In the process of throwing, your back foot should leave the chair and finish the pitch. The front landing foot can be shortened until you feel the extension.

- **Inconsistent leg kick or sweeping:** Start in the pivot position with leg-kick leg lifted. Place the lift foot on a chair. Start the drill by lifting the foot off the chair up to your waist and head directly to the plate. Lifting the foot off the chair should help develop a consistent leg kick.

Heading directly to the plate should eliminate a leg sweep. This drill can be done on the mound or flat ground.

A pitcher has only one usable arm. When this arm is injured or permanently disabled, his career is slowed or over. It is very important to take care of the pitching arm, especially the young pitcher's. In the following pages I will discuss how to stay in shape and approximately how many pitches should be thrown at once. As a rule of thumb, a pitcher should receive one day off for each 30 pitches thrown in a game. If a pitcher is under the age of 15, he needs more rest to avoid injury.

Figure 118. Dead front side

30 pitches = one day off
60 pitches = two days off
90 pitches = three days off

It is important not to throw much more than 90 pitches in a game. If a pitcher throws 90-plus pitches, a four-

Figure 119. Spread drill

Figure 120.
Chair drill

day rest is recommended. A young pitcher should not throw more than 50 or 60. This may not sound like many, but remember: In order to get loose for the game, the pitcher threw an additional 40 to 60 or more pitches. This does not show up on the pitch count, but the arm does not know the difference. A pitcher should try to loosen up for at least 12 to 15 minutes prior to starting a game. The idea is to be good and loose, and a bit sweaty.

Indoor Practice and Drills

Because so many areas of the country have to start the baseball season in the gym, it is important to cover some aspects of the game that can be practiced indoors. Most of the common problem drills can be done inside also.

Every coach knows the importance of a pitcher throwing strikes. Unfortunately, a pitcher cannot throw off the mound at full speed every day, and in some instances no mound for pitching is available. In these cases, a pitcher can work on command with a variety of drills. The most important thing to remember when doing the drill is that the pitcher needs to take the work seriously.

TARGET THROWING WITH A PARTNER

Toss-and-catch seems to be a mindless drill; many people think it serves only to loosen the arm and kill time. This is not the frame of mind the pitcher should take. Toss-and-catch is the perfect time to work through the windup and delivery and concentrate on proper arm action and angle, as well as on target throwing. You and a partner should set up about 40 to 60 feet apart. The partner should squat like a catcher and create a good target before you start the motion. Take your time; as with any drill, rushing or working incorrectly will only create bad habits. A mound is not necessary; a line on the floor or a piece of tape to mark the rubber is fine. Work on throwing to different spots, not just the middle of the chest. All pitches can be worked on here.

STATUE DRILL

The statue drill can be of help for the pitcher who has problems with his balance point. It can also help all pitchers regain a solid balance point before starting the season. Start in the stretch. From here, lift the leg into the leg kick, stop, and stay there (see Figure 121). At this point the arm should start the arc, and the front arm should extend out in front of the body pointing directly at the target. This is the

Figure 121. Statue position

statue position. Continue the rest of the delivery, throwing to targets. This drill will help you develop a feel for the balance point. It may also isolate the arm action and leg kick, making it easier to find the proper leg-kick height for each individual. In the latter case (see Figure 122), keep in mind that the loaded position should be achieved at the point the landing foot hits the ground. The fastball and change-up are most effective in this drill, but all pitches can be used.

DRY DRILL

As you know, a pitcher can only throw 50 to 100 pitches every three or four days. Early in the year, especially indoors, 20 to 40 pitches is about all a pitcher can throw in a two-day period, because he is not in shape. These few pitches are not enough time to work on mechanics, as well as release, arm action, angle, and everything else a delivery requires. The dry drill is an opportunity to work on the mechanics part of the windup and delivery without throwing a ball. A pitcher can do these every day, and hundreds at a time, if necessary. This drill is very easy to do, but it can cause big problems if done incorrectly.

Use a partner or a mirror to monitor progress. Start in the address portion of the windup. From here, run through the whole windup and delivery. You can stop at certain problem points of the delivery, or continue a dry run of proper mechanics from start to finish. Working out of the windup

Figure 122. Load at landing

and stretch is helpful. This drill is extremely helpful both early in the season with the arm out of shape and for the pitcher who has mechanical problems.

MIRROR WORK

This practice drill helps a pitcher visualize what is right and wrong with his own windup, delivery, arm action, and arm angle. Instead of hearing from the coach day in and day out all the things he is doing wrong, he can see them himself. A mound is not a must, but it is helpful in this drill. If no mound is available, again put a strip of tape on the floor parallel with the wall the mirror is on. If you do have a mound, place it facing the mirror so the pitcher can see. As time goes on, the mound or tape will need to be moved so the pitcher can see himself from the side as well as the front.

Run through the windup, delivery, arm action, stretch—any part of the pitcher's action desired—without a ball. Make corrections so the pitcher can see what is right and wrong—and the difference between the two. Eventually the pitcher will be able to run this drill himself, making corrections and doing many reps.

FIELDING THE POSITION

An indoor mound is not necessary for this drill; in fact, mounds are steep and make it very easy for the pitcher to get injured. Rather than a regulation baseball, use a softer ball of the standard size and weight to help save the gym floor and reduce the chance of injury—the background and lighting are not always the best.

Start by having the pitcher stand 40 to 50 feet away from the hitter. Have the pitcher run through the pitching motion and finish just as if he were throwing the ball. At release, the hitter should hit the ball and the pitcher work on fielding the ball. He can also practice his footwork and pivot to the bases, and work on fielding bunts. If the area is large enough to have simulated bases, have other players cover bases and act as base runners while you work on situations. The important thing is that the pitcher go through the proper mechanics of the delivery and the process of throwing to the bases.

Other things can be done with this workout. The pitcher can work on covering first when a ball is hit to the right side. If you can cover this drill indoors, it will allow you to work on other things when you get outside.

BAREHAND WORK

A pitcher needs good hand–eye coordination to field a ball hit back at the mound. Most of the time when he misses those plays, it is because he tenses up at the point when the ball reaches the glove. This may not be the pitcher's fault. Many times the ball looks to be hit harder than it really is, and sometimes it is hit so hard that he has no time to prepare himself. This drill may help a pitcher relax when fielding, and may also give him more confidence in his hands than he has now.

Start by having the pitcher stand 35 to 50 feet away from the hitter; he does not use his glove in this drill. Be sure to use a soft baseball. Many softballs that are regulation size and weight are available today at sporting goods shops; a tennis ball will also do just fine. After the pitcher runs through the windup and delivery and finishes the action, hit the ball back at him. He should now field it without the use of his glove, getting more comfortable with using his hands. Later, when he puts his glove back on, his hand will seem much larger—and his fielding should improve.

SLIDE DRILL OR PICKUPS

This drill is designed to help in conditioning as well as improving the pitcher's hand–eye coordination and bunt fielding. Two players partner up and stand approximately 6 to 8 feet apart, facing each other. One player should have two balls in his hand. These balls can be regulation; they can be soft or hard, or even tennis balls. The player with the balls rolls one ball to his left, about 5 feet to the side of the pitcher; do not roll hard. The pitcher needs to shuffle, not run, after the ball. As soon as he picks up the rolled ball, the partner should roll the other ball approximately 5 feet to the other side. As he does so, the pitcher tosses the first ball underhand to his partner, then shuffles over to pick up the second ball, as the partner rolls the first ball to the left again.

Here are some tips for this drill. The pitcher should pick up the ball with the hand that is on the outside of the roll. For instance, if he is shuffling to the left, he should use his left hand. He should also underhand toss the ball to his partner with his left hand. If he is moving to the right, he should pick up the ball and underhand toss with the right hand. When the required number of pickups is achieved, the two partners can switch roles. For fun, sometimes a game can be made out of the drill. See how many times the pitcher can successfully pick up the rolled ball and complete the play by making an accurate throw. Then have the other player do the same. Do not stop when a play is mishandled; just start over until the desired number of pickups is completed. Sometimes a time limit is introduced, and the pitcher picks up as many balls as possible in that limit (see Figures 123–125).

Many drills are of importance indoors, but it is sometimes overlooked that in a game a pitcher needs to execute even when exhausted. This drill will help train him to work while very tired.

OFF-SPEED DRILLS

If a pitcher is working on a change-up and needs to get a feel for this pitch's grip and release, the box drill is helpful. Tape a strike zone on the wall of the gym. After putting the square on the wall, add two more lines. The first extends from the middle of the box across the center to the

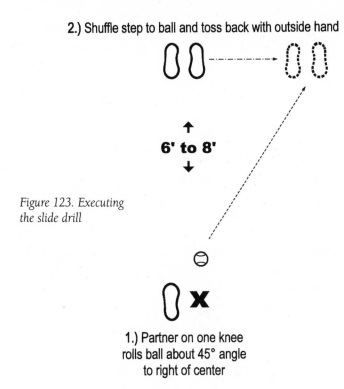

2.) Shuffle step to ball and toss back with outside hand

↑
6' to 8'
↓

Figure 123. Executing the slide drill

1.) Partner on one knee
rolls ball about 45° angle
to right of center

middle of the other side. Add the second strip of tape from the middle of the top of the box down to the middle of the bottom line. The box is now split into four sections (see Figure 126). The pitcher stands 35 to 40 feet away. If an indoor mound is available, by all means use it, but if not put a tape line on the floor to serve as a rubber. Using the change-up grip, the pitcher should work on the windup delivery and throw to a certain section inside the box. The idea is to concentrate on the release and arm speed to correctly execute the change. Continue to work on this until it feels comfortable and accuracy improves.

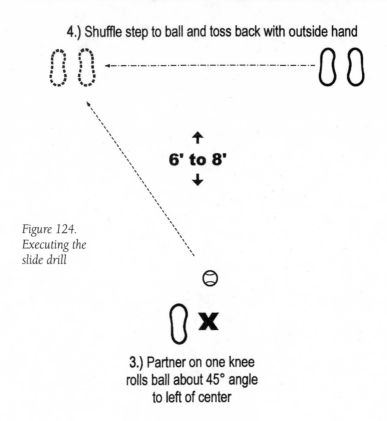

4.) Shuffle step to ball and toss back with outside hand

6' to 8'

Figure 124. Executing the slide drill

3.) Partner on one knee
rolls ball about 45° angle
to left of center

This drill will not really help the curveball: The distance is not far enough for the action of the curveball to happen. If you can move the mound back to 60 feet, however, working on the curve is possible. If no mound is available, do not work this drill with the curveball. Remember, though, not to throw too many curveballs. It is very easy to throw 40 or 50 curveballs—and this is *not* a good idea. In this drill, 10 or 20 curveballs is the maximum for one session; do not repeat for at least two days. The young pitcher should not be using the curveball at all.

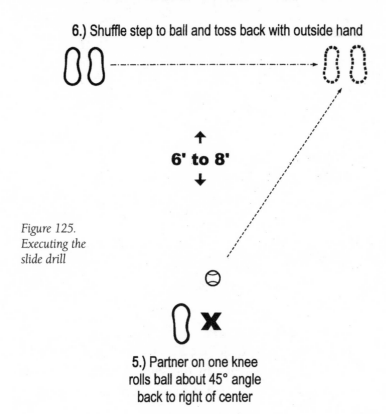

6.) Shuffle step to ball and toss back with outside hand

↑
6' to 8'
↓

Figure 125.
Executing the
slide drill

5.) Partner on one knee
rolls ball about 45° angle
back to right of center

To work on the slider, a mound is necessary for proper execution. The mound needs to be at least 45 feet from the box, but 60 feet is recommended. Again, do not use this drill for more than 10 or 20 sliders in a workout. And as with the curveball, take two days off before repeating the drill. If you are simply working the fastball or change-up, this drill can be done every other day with 40 to 50 repetitions, as long as they are not full speed—effort should not exceed 50 or 60 percent.

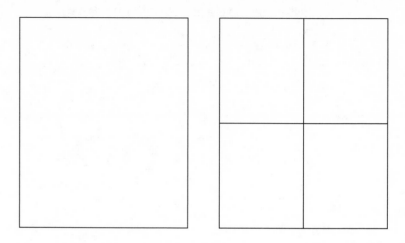

Figure 126. Box drill

This drill can be conducted outdoors just as easily by marking or taping a fence in the same design. A colored string can be used to thread through a chain-link fence to create the box.

ONE-KNEE DRILL

The one-knee drill helps develop both the change and the fastball. Start with the back knee or balance leg on the floor or ground. The landing foot should be out in front of the body at a point where the foot can be flat on the floor, while still feeling comfortable. If the foot is too far out in front, it will make balance very hard to achieve. If it is too close to the body, the hips will not turn correctly. The foot should be toes in as discussed in chapter 1. Have a partner stand facing the pitcher about 30 to 35 feet away.

The pitcher throws with proper grip and his hands together at his hips out in front of his body. From here, break the hands correctly, and execute the arm action and angle as well as the front glove action. The meat and potatoes of this drill is to correctly work on the change (see Figure 127). With the grip and hand action correct, throw the ball to the partner with enough arm speed to make the pitch look like a fastball when in reality it is an off-speed pitch.

Here are some things to work on in this drill. The glove should extend to the target and pull back to the chest. Be sure the grip and arm action are performed correctly. If done right, control and a feel for the change will be developed. Using this drill for the slider is also fine because this pitch has to do with finish of the wrist and fingers. The curveball is not recommended, however: Without the use of the lower body, the curveball will not work correctly. It requires the incline of the mound and the lower body for its finish.

Figure 127. One-knee drill

SPREAD DRILL

This drill can aid in the upper body, and can also help practice the push-off and work the pitcher's glove action. It may also clean up the arm angle or finish. Start by putting the back foot parallel to a line on the floor or strip of tape. This will simulate the rubber. If a mound is available, use it (see Figure 128). Place your landing foot in the area close to where it would land on a mound. At this point, the legs should be spread well apart. Be sure to place the landing foot in a position where it is pointed at your partner, who is receiving the ball. Remember to place the foot in the toed-in position. The hand and glove should be together at the waist.

The partner should stand approx-imately 40 feet away. Do not stand farther apart than this, because the upper body and lower body are separated and the arm will end up throwing a long distance. Also, throwing from a flat surface will put extra pressure on the shoulder. This drill is fine for all pitches, but the fastball and change-up are recommended. Be sure not to work on too many mechanics. Concentrate on one or two and save the others for the next workout, or until the first are mastered. Make sure to complete the action of both body and arm or the drill will do more harm than good.

Figure 128 . Spread drill

From the position described above, break the hand and start the arm action, properly executing the arm action and angle as well as running through the front-hand action. Pay attention to proper grip and throw. Regardless of the pitch, this drill should help clean up the delivery and get a feel for the pitch.

This drill can be combined with the box drill; no second player is needed. If a mound is available, it is recommended; if not, this drill can still be used for the fastball and change-up, and maybe the slider. (The curveball needs the incline of the mound.) With any pitch other than the fastball or change-up, do not exceed 10 or 20 throws at a time. With the fastball or change-up, 30 to 50 reps is fine, as long as proper rest is given before repeating this drill.

BACK-OF-THE-MOUND DRILL

This drill is designed for the pitcher who is having problems throwing downhill. Start by having the pitcher stand behind the mound (see Figure 129). The catcher needs to move up from home plate about 15 feet and squat in position. The pitcher now puts his landing foot up on the mound, just behind the rubber. The back foot should be turned to simulate being in front of the rubber after the pivot. With the proper arm action, he throws to the catcher. This should help the pitcher feel the downhill action needed. After a few throws, return to the mound and throw to the catcher. Repeat as necessary.

WALL DRILL

This drill is for the pitcher having problems with the arc. If a pitcher is extending the arc too far behind his body,

Figure 129. Back-of-the-mound drill

this drill should help correct it. Have him stand with his back against a wall. Now start the motion from the stretch and simulate a throw. If his arc is too long, his hand will hit the wall. With the wall behind the pitcher, he will be conscious of the problem and shorten the arc to the correct position.

FOOTBALL THROW

For the pitcher working on his slider, throwing a football is of help. This simulates the slider release very closely. This may also help you learn the cutter. Be sure not to throw hard or for a long distance. Just concentrate on the feeling of the wrist at release. The pitcher who is having problems shortening his arc may also find the football throw helpful, because a football is very difficult to throw with an arc.

These are a few drills that should help you master the art of pitching. There are hundreds more than can be done. But do remember that the most important part of any drill—no matter what it is designed to do—is correctly performing it. Doing a drill incorrectly is worse than not doing it at all. If you cannot take a serious approach, then do not do the drill at all.

Conditioning

There are many parts to the windup, delivery, and finish. There are equally as many things to remember when it comes to grip, arm action, and angle. But there is also a part of pitching that, if left unattended, will cause all of the other work to be worthless. The conditioning part of the pitcher's program is just as important as his mechanics—if not more important—because if an injury occurs, whether to the arm, shoulders, legs, or back, it will be very hard to perform any mechanics.

Every pitcher is different, so as I discuss the following programs and activities, be aware that it will take time to figure which activities work for *you*. A player with a strong upper body may need to concentrate on his lower half, for instance—or vice versa. And regardless which part of the body is underdeveloped, the arm must always be attended to. When working on these drills, always take time to work on the arm and shoulder, too, because this is the most fragile part of the pitcher's body.

Below is a regular schedule for the pitcher. This schedule is designed for the pitcher who does nothing but pitch for his team. Most pitchers, of course, play another position in addition to the pitching two times a week. For them, a revised schedule is offered.

Pitching Only, Five-Day Rotation

Day 1. Pitch game.

Day 2. Run distance; 2 to 3 miles is enough. If poles are substituted, run 16 to 20 poles.

Day 3. Run; lightly toss until loose; a short session of long toss; sprints of 40 to 60 yards, 15 repetitions.

Day 4. Short session of pitching off the mound at 75 percent for command; run 1 to 2 miles or 12 to 15 poles.

Day 5. Ten to 15 sprints; run 8 to 10 poles or 1 mile.

Day 6. Pitch again.

Pitcher–Position Player

Day 1. Pitch game.

Day 2. Play some light toss. Get the arm loose, but do not tax it by throwing hard. Before the game, run 10 to 12 sprints.

Day 3. Try to get a distance run or pole work done; if possible, a light 50 percent work on mound.

Day 4. Ten to 12 sprints and 8 poles; a brief long toss.

Day 5. Rest arm; 10 sprints.

Day 6. Pitch again.

Long toss and throwing off the mound may be switched, based on how the arm feels. Be sure to incorporate work on the mound, though. If long toss is impossible between starts, plug in some extra mound work. During the mound sessions, do not throw more than 10 curveballs, sliders, or cutters. Be sure to work on the change-up—15 to 20 pitches. Do not exceed 50 pitches during the workout. This would mean maybe five of every pitch, and the rest fastballs.

IN SEASON

Lifting once a week is no problem during the season, but do not lift on pitching day, and do not try to gain size until the season is over. Light weights with lots of repetitions is the idea. Any weight that cannot be lifted at least 12 times is too heavy. The idea is to maintain strength and stay loose, not muscle bound. Be sure to not neglect the shoulder and arm.

OFF SEASON

Lifting three days a week is fine. If you are alternating upper- and lower-body days, lifting every day is fine. The idea in the off season is to work hard to develop the weaker parts of the body. It is still important to stay loose. Medium weights with lots of repetitions is still recommended. If a weight cannot be lifted 10 times, it should be lightened.

Be sure to work on the shoulders and arms. The difference between the season and the off season when it comes to the arm and shoulders is that in the off season, additional work must be done to keep them loose—light throwing or extensive stretching. If the arm and shoulder are neglected at this time of year, the muscles and tendons will stiffen, and an injury is sure to follow.

RECOMMENDED EXERCISES

Below is a list of exercises that can be performed both in and out of season, but be sure to adjust the workout according to the time of year. Also keep in mind that in the off season, an extensive running program of both distances and sprints should be incorporated.

For Legs
- Squats
- Leg extensions
- Leg curl
- Groin exercises
- Running distances
- Sprints
- Jumping rope

For Upper Body
- Bench press
- Military press
- Curls
- Lateral pull-downs
- Sit-ups
- Incline bench

- Lightweight shoulder exercises
- Flies
- Oblique work
- Push-ups

POLES

The pole drill involves starting by the foul pole in the outfield corner and running along the fence to the other foul pole. There are many ways it can be executed. You can sprint to the opposite alley: If you're starting in the right-field corner, run to the left center-field gap, walk to the left-field foul pole, then run to the right center-field gap, and walk to the right-field pole. If you are counting, this is two poles. Another way to run the poles is to run from one pole to another and rest for one minute, then return to the first pole and rest there for one minute. Again, this is two poles. Or you can run to the nearest gap at full speed, walk to the other gap, and walk to the foul line. Turn around, sprint to the nearest gap, walk to the next gap, and sprint full speed to the foul line. Again—two poles.

FOOTBALL PASSES

Running poles can become boring, and pitchers get tired of the same work every day. A running drill that will help pitchers enjoy getting in shape is the football pass. Have the coach, a position player, or even a trainer stand in center field, about medium depth. Have each pitcher bring a ball and form a line at the foul line near the warning track or fence. The first pitcher runs at a good pace and direct line to the person in center field. When he reaches the person, he lightly tosses him the ball. Then he begins to run full speed to the foul line opposite where he started—like a wide receiver. The person in center lets him run 30 or 40 yards and then leads him with a throw that the pitcher tries to catch. After he catches or retrieves the ball, he should form a line at the foul line in that field. As each player completes the drill, he should fall in line behind the first pitcher.

Keep up a good pace. As the pitcher gets halfway to the person in center field, the second pitcher should follow. When the first pitcher is catching his pass, the second should be reaching the person in center field to repeat the drill. As the second pitcher gets halfway, the third pitcher starts. At the end of the line, when the last pitcher has started his run to catch the throw, the first pitcher starts running—and the drill begins again.

POSTSCRIPT

Pitching is the most important part of baseball. It is also the most complicated position to learn. In order to be a productive pitcher, you will have to spend many hours perfecting the motion and arm action. Keep in mind while you practice the position that any single action you can perfect will help you become a better pitcher. Perfecting all the mechanics, however, is impossible.

Every pitcher is different. Just because one pitcher has trouble with a certain movement does not mean that all pitchers will struggle with it. Concentrate on your own mechanics and find out how to fix your particular problems. Velocity is nice. Movement is also important, but when getting hitters out, a combination of location, life, and velocity is most effective. Throw the ball over the plate, stay ahead in the count, and you should not have any problems.